Praise for *S*

changing our thinking is possible. *Sweet Sharing*, indeed!

Linda Quiring, author of *Island of Knowledge*

"Ankush Jain's book *Sweet Sharing* makes for sweet reading. Throughout the book Ankush sprinkles stories, anecdotes, and nuggets of wisdom that bring us back to our childlike sense of wonder and show us that our well-being, love, and resilience are always within us."

Amir Karkouti, author of *What the F**k are the Three Principles? and 18 Other Questions from So-Called Wisdom*

"This is a great book full of helpful examples drawn from the author's own life, that will help you have your own insights about how the mind works. It's clear, simple and packed with everyday wisdom that anyone can benefit from."

Chantal Burns, author of the #1 bestseller *Instant Motivation: The surprising truth behind what drives top performance* and Founder of www.consciousleadershipschool.com

"*Sweet Sharing* is an insightful and moving portrayal of a very human life that we all can see ourselves in. Maybe *Sweet Sharing* can help us reflect on our own lives with a more compassionate lens, thus allowing us a greater lightness of being. This is the story of "everyman". Thank you, Ankush, for sharing your human journey.

Catherine Casey, M.A., Clinical Psychology
Principle Based Consultant

"Through stories, insights and simple practices, *Sweet Sharing* allows you, the reader, a look inside your own mind. The chance to see and better understand your own thinking and feelings and how both, for better or worse, create your reality. Whatever you are looking for in life, these ideas are invaluable in helping you find it."

David Schwendiman, author of *Selling from the Top of the Ladder: The Ultimate Sales Playbook*

"*Sweet Sharing* takes the reader on a journey of rediscovery.

Ankush brings us his own personal journey while creating the space for us to wake up to the true nature of ourselves. This honest, vulnerable, and inspiring look at life will leave the reader ready to tap into their own source of unlimited power."

Devon Bandison, author of *Fatherhood Is Leadership: Your Playbook for Success, Self-Leadership, and a Richer Life*

"Ankush has done an amazing job weaving together the tapestry of his life and his current understanding of how the mind really works. The stories throughout are real, relevant, and help connect the dots for those of us just starting to see how state of mind impacts one's life. He so eloquently and clearly points to living more authentically and harmoniously. A must read!"

Sherry Welsh, author of *Slowing Down: Unexpected Ways to Thrive as a Female Leader*

"Ankush Jain has written an insightful book about how we all tell ourselves stories about who we think we are and then believe them to be true. Using his personal experience Ankush provides hope to people who have been seduced by their own stories. By simply understanding how these inner narratives work, they can live lives of unlimited joy and inner peace."

Chana Studley, author of *The Myth of Low Self Esteem: A Novel about PTSD, Hollywood, and Healing*

Simple, fresh and direct, Ankush Jain's book is packed with stories and truths that reawaken us to who we truly are and always have been and how, when we begin to understand the nature of our inner world, life gets easier, richer and sweeter. Jain makes simple and digestible what our overactive minds make confusing and complex. A must-read book for all.

Melissa Ford, co-author of *When All Boats Rise: 12 Coaches on Service as the Heart of a Thriving Practice*

"I've often thought how great it would be if when we were born, we all came with a manual that told us how life works, how we create our experience, how the equipment of the mind works. How much easier things could be for us. *Sweet Sharing* comes pretty close to being that manual. Ankush explores the full range of the human experience—from insecurity and boredom to the darker realities of racism and anger—not as abstract concepts, but by sharing his own deeply personal stories. This book is real, honest, vulnerable, and compelling. Here is your life's manual."

Linda Ford, coach and author of *Women and Confidence: The Truth About the Lies We Tell Ourselves*

"As you read *Sweet Sharing* you will be greeted by the essence of Kush. He shares wisdom effortlessly, simply and poetically. This allows for a gentle heart tug to greet you and allow you to see things as you have never seen them before, feel things in a new way and be with yourself in a kinder, gentler way."

Gary Mahler, co-author of *When All Boats Rise: 12 Coaches on Service as the Heart of a Thriving Practice*

"In this powerhouse of a book, Ankush shares an amazing story full of insights into what it means to be human. *Sweet Sharing* offers you a front-row seat on his journey through false beliefs and misunderstandings to a rediscovery of himself. I highly recommend this book to anyone who is ready to wake up to who they really are."

Laurie Holmes, author of *Becoming Human: The Story of You and Me and How We Came to Be*

"Join Ankush in a sincere and open exploration of who he really is, and also who *you* really are. *Sweet Sharing* is a journey of self-discovery that may relieve you of the baggage you thought you really needed.

Henk Kok, author of *The Deep Peace of Living in the Feeling*

"Sweet Sharing hits the right note. It's a sweetly satisfying read that isn't saccharine. Through stories of his own journey, Ankush takes us by the hand and gently leads us to see life through fresh eyes, to a place of transformation and joy."

Elaine Hildes, author of *MindFullness: The No-Diet Diet Book*

SWEET SHARING
Rediscovering the REAL You

SWEET SHARING
Rediscovering the REAL You

Ankush Jain

Sweet Sharing

Copyright © 2019 by Ankush Jain

Published by Ankush Jain Publishing

Contact the author:
ankush@ankushjain.co.uk
www.ankushjain.co.uk

Editing and layout by Chris Nelson
Cover design by Brent Atkinson

ISBN: 9781796646832

A CIP record for this book is available from the British Library

First Edition

~ To all my clients,
past, present and future ~

Table of Contents

Foreword by Steve Chandler...xiii

1. When Does Your Story Begin?............................... 3
2. The Early Years 6
3. My Lowest Point and a Glimmer of Hope................... 8
4. An Introduction to Personal Development 10
5. Looking for a Feeling Through Alcohol and Partying........ 12
6. The Start of a New Career 15
7. Insights Around Time Management 19
8. Anger and Road Rage 22
9. Going Deeper.. 25
10. Is Forgiveness Really Necessary?....................... 29
11. Is Acceptance Necessary?.............................. 32
12. My Feeling Guilty Was Not Indicative of a Conscience 34
13. Can Fear and Love Coexist?............................ 37
14. Comparison Is a Mind Virus............................ 40
15. You Don't Need to Change Your Thinking............... 43
16. The Feeling of Love for Your Spouse 46
17. Gut Instincts and Insights............................. 49
18. The Power of Silence.................................. 53
19. You Are Not Who You Think You Are.................... 57
20. Difficult People Don't Exist 60
21. The Illogic of the Comfort Zone....................... 63
22. Are You the Average of the People You Hang
    Around With?.. 67
23. There Are No Exceptions.............................. 70
24. Wisdom and Common Sense Are the Same 72
25. You Always Have a Choice............................. 75
26. Why Is Making a Change So Difficult?................. 78
27. The Real Cause of Complaining 81
28. Beating Yourself Up 84
29. A Different Take on Procrastination.................... 87
30. The Real Source of Stress............................. 90

31. You Don't Need Motivation 93
32. Your Thinking Isn't a Problem 96
33. Owner Versus Victim 99
34. Being Powerful from Within 101
35. Fear Is not a Problem 104
36. You can Change Your Mind 108
37. Ego Is Made of Thought 111
38. Dealing with Criticism 114
39. Your Own Capacity/Potential 117
40. You Can Have What You Want 120
41. Racism Is No Exception 123
42. Planning (Is It Necessary?) 126
43. The Media Innocently Promotes Misunderstanding 129
44. Don't Give Your Power Away 133
45. What Happens when You're Offended? 135
46. Generosity Is Innate 138
47. Can Money Make You Unhappy? 141
48. Hard Work Doesn't Have to Be Hard 144
49. You Don't Need to Be Appreciated 147
50. You Are Resilient by Design 151
51. Why? 154
52. Fasting and Giving Up Luxuries 157
53. The Flow State Is Here, Now 159
54. You Don't Need to Avoid Boredom 161
55. Love from Our Parents 163
56. Listening Is Easy 166
57. How Do I Stop Thinking? 168
58. The Promise of a Life Lived from
    a New Understanding 171

Acknowledgements 173
Further Reading 175
About the Author 177

He Is Giving You Everything

Ankush Jain has been a brilliant coach and teacher for a number of years, and I have had the pleasure of co-facilitating seminars with him online and in London, England. With a career like his there was really no need for him to take the time and make the effort to write a book—especially a book as powerful and personal as this one.

I've read this book twice: first a number of months ago in its original draft form, and now again in its final, beautifully-finished form. Each time I was moved and touched, not just by his positive philosophy of life and the principles behind it, but even more by the moving personal experiences he shares so sweetly.

It caused me to recall a testimonial blurb on the cover of a book I read and loved decades ago. The book was *The Road Less Traveled* by M. Scott Peck. And the review was by Phyllis Theroux of *The Washington Post*, and she said, "Not just a book, but a spontaneous act of generosity."

That's this book.

To answer the question, "What's it about?" I might turn to the very last chapter, entitled "The Promise of a Life Lived from a New Understanding." That's the exact promise this book actually delivers on.

Ankush presents this new understanding by sharing experiences. Not only his own difficult experiences of life—made all the more painful by his lack of understanding of how his mind worked, the role of thought in his life and the existence of universal consciousness as his true, loving identity.

(And who understands those things early in life anyway, if ever?)

But he also shares the experiences of his clients, who showed him that the understanding this book offers us is teachable, coachable, translatable, deliverable, and available to everyone—not just the lucky few who have had spontaneous enlightenment experiences.

What sets this book apart from so many others that seek to be guides to personal transformation is that the messages here are not laid out as prescriptive actions, as steps you should take or concepts and theories for you to try to believe in. This book is pure sharing. This makes it easy to enjoy and reflect on. It's hard to argue with someone's real-life experience.

There are no opinions in this book. There is nothing you have to agree or disagree with. There are simply, throughout, the moving and touching stories and confessions of a young man trying to succeed. These real-life stories—amusing, painful and inspiring as they are—eventually become an offering to the reader, out of pure generosity, of a new understanding.

As the book unfolds the reader experiences right alongside the author how this understanding opens life up to more love and more light and more creativity.

Ankush's life changed when he attended a three-day seminar conducted by Jamie Smart and featuring Garret Kramer. Both Smart and Kramer were distinguished authors and coaches who taught the principles behind Mind, Thought and Consciousness. For the first time in his life Ankush caught a quick but unforgettable glimpse into the true source of his emotional struggles with anger.   This was when what he calls "the understanding" began to reveal itself in his life.

I especially love Ankush's chapter about time management. Even though he took courses and learned useful tools for prioritization of activities, the real breakthrough came by observing his own mind and its thoughts. He noticed his anger when interrupted by annoying emails. But now, with his new understanding, instead of acting on the anger by lashing out or complaining to his co-workers, he wonders, "What if my angry feelings aren't telling me how much of an idiot the person sending the email is? What if the angry feelings aren't telling me how justified I am in sending back a short, sharp response?"

What if, he asks, they are only telling him about his own thoughts?

The full import of the insights he got in the seminar on coaching from the principles behind mind, thought and consciousness—the "understanding"—was now showing up in his daily life. What he had seen could not be unseen. He says, "As I stopped getting sidetracked by emails which I thought were causing me to feel angry, I started getting more time back in my day. What a gift!"

The book continues from there, reading like an adventure story, as we follow Ankush ascending his learning curve. Like the light from an early sunrise beginning to filter through a forest, his life gets lighter and brighter, little by little, day by day. Each chapter gently leads us by the hand through the distribution of that light and shows how Ankush eventually took that deep feeling of "What a gift!" into the profession of teaching and coaching—so that others could share in that gift.

The words of the poet Robert Graves come to my mind:

> Giving you everything,
> I too, who once had nothing,
> Am left with more than everything

I am so happy this book is in the world now; it is a gift to all of us. I say this even having already benefitted so much from the *Relationship Series* Ankush created and put up on YouTube for everyone. In it, he interviews many of the distinguished teachers, psychologists and coaches who teach the same understanding Ankush was introduced to by Jamie Smart, Garret Kramer and later more deeply by Dr Keith Blevens. Many of my own clients are asked to listen to that series, especially if they have relationship problems, all of which seem to be some version of Ankush's own misunderstandings of where his angry feelings were actually coming from.

As if that series weren't enough, Ankush Jain has also been an active presence on social media, offering his insights and video-coaching sessions at no charge for the rapidly-growing number of people who are *waking up* by following him.

He also does live immersion groups and seminars, and as someone invited to co-facilitate with him, I've been able to experience his skill and quiet grace at sharing the gift up close and personal.

This book, however, takes all of this into a new dimension. It gives us the full story, what I will call (and he'd never call) a *hero's journey*. In his choice of words, this is simply a journey from misunderstanding to understanding. *Sweet Sharing* gives us a way to walk that journey with him, all the way from beginning to end. Or, rather, from beginning to where he is now. Because when you get a sense of the infinite nature of the "understanding"—and you will if you read this book slowly—you'll feel that this journey has no end.

Which is why I can't wait for the next book authored by Ankush Jain. He is one writer who knows how to put his life into words, and I look forward to learning even more about what he experiences as a gifted teacher of the insights in the book. His words near the end are a sweet sharing of what his life is now about:

"I have seen so many lives changed beyond what people thought possible that I know the potential exists for *everyone* . . . If my life can change to the degree that it has, then I know it is absolutely possible for everyone else."

All I can say to that, and to Ankush, is: Wow. Thanks so much for your gift of such an aptly-titled book.

Steve Chandler
February, 2019
Birmingham, Michigan

CHAPTER 1.

When Does Your Story Begin?

I thought my story began when I was nine or ten years old.

At that time my parents loved hosting family and friends at our house in the suburbs of Walsall, a town in the centre of England. I remember that whenever people visited, whether I had met them already or not, I would be incredibly shy and scared to talk with them. I would stand there, not answering questions and staring at my feet.

My parents commented on this, telling me, "Boys aren't shy." But I couldn't help how I felt, so I took that on as my personality: I was forevermore a shy person.

I thought my story started there and carried on through my teenage years into my twenties, when I discovered the self-help and personal development world. Then, by taking deliberate steps outside of what many would describe as my "comfort zone," I started to show up more confidently in life, both personally and professionally. This wasn't a dramatic change but one that seemed to involve numerous small steps over many years. If you had told me back then that one day I would write a book about my journey I would have guessed it would contain the step-by-step path I took from shy boy to confident adult.

However, a few years ago I had a revelatory insight that showed me my story didn't start when I was nine or ten years old. In fact, it began much earlier.

What happened was that I suddenly recalled a memory of an

event that had taken place when I was far younger in Mumbai, India. My family and I had gone to visit our relatives. One day we were at my uncle's apartment. He lived in a colony, which is a group of tall apartment buildings surrounded by a wall. While I was visiting my uncle, he took me to another apartment in the colony to meet his friend. My memory is a little hazy, but I remember meeting a young lady there who was perhaps in her late teens or early twenties. In an innocent, childlike way I remember that I liked her and decided that she was now my friend.

After meeting her, my uncle and I walked back to his apartment. A little while later, as we were getting ready to leave, my sister and I were given some sweets by my uncle as a parting gift. I distinctly remember refusing to leave unless I could share my sweets with my new friend.

My family tried in vain to convince me that the sweets were mine but I wouldn't have it. I forced my uncle to march me across to my new friend's apartment so I could share my sweets with her. I remember feeling so excited as I waited for her to open the door. She was really surprised when we turned up. There was such joy in her eyes when this small child told her he wanted to share his sweets with her.

In that moment I certainly wasn't shy. I didn't lack confidence. I didn't have a problem connecting with women and I certainly wasn't overanalysing the situation. I was my true self—unfiltered. I was free of all the mistaken beliefs about who I was, the ones I picked up in subsequent years.

In these pages I share insights and stories that I hope will help you remember who *you* are—once you drop your own false beliefs, misconceptions and misunderstandings—and to understand the value of this remembering. It frees you up to live without your insecurities and doubts holding you back. It helps you return to the state of childlike creativity, playfulness and joy we all once had.

One is never quite sure what will make this new understanding "click." I have found it useful on my own journey to gently reflect on the many areas of our lives where it comes into play—namely *everywhere*. This is what we'll do in this book. If it seems on occasion that we've already touched on a particular issue, I invite you to reflect on it anew. Oftentimes when we look at the same or similar problems from different angles, we nurture a deeper understanding that leads to growth.

I have spent some eighteen years exploring self-development and learning from some of the best teachers, mentors and coaches on the planet, as well as coaching others towards the insights in this book. I'm also simply a guy whose experience of life was pretty average at best but who underwent some pretty huge transformations as I began to understand what I share with you in the following pages. The extent of these changes has been miraculous to me. Before them I simply could not imagine enjoying life as much as I do now.

But this book isn't really about my transformation. Rather it's about remembering who I really was back then—and who I always have been, for that matter.

This remembering is possible for everyone.

When does *your* story begin?

CHAPTER 2.

The Early Years

I soon forgot about the sharing of my sweets. The innocent, kind, generous and happy young Ankush became a distant memory. The first big shift happened when I was six years old. My parents, keen to give me the best start in life, enrolled me in the prestigious local private school, which had a reputation for offering an excellent education.

I'll never forget my first day. The school was a converted manor house with large grounds—very different from my previous school. My mum packed me off with whatever she thought I needed and I nervously embarked on this new adventure.

My first day didn't go quite as planned. At one point my teacher pulled me out of class and shouted at me in the corridor for not having any coloured pencils with me; I only had felt-tip pens. Discipline here was certainly important to the teachers.

That year my grades were close to the bottom of the class. This was surprising to my parents, since in my previous school they had been the opposite. In fact, the teachers at my old school would complain that I finished my work too quickly and bothered the other children. I still remember my old head teacher wishing me well when I left to go to the private school. That first year at my new school I'm sure I wished I could go back.

For the next five years, it seemed my life had only one goal: to pass my "11-plus" entrance exams, which determined whether I would go to the local comprehensive school or whether I was clever enough to attend a selective grammar school in Birmingham. The ultimate aim was to pass the exams to attend a selective independent school, deemed one of the top in the country. To that end, I received private tuition on top of my school work to ensure I got the grades I needed.

School life wasn't much fun. There were twenty-four children in my class, and I still remember when one kid had a birthday party where he invited the entire class but one: me. Perhaps that's why, years later, I tried so hard to be popular. I hated that feeling of being left out, of not being good enough and not belonging.

I don't want to give the impression that life was terrible. I had a family who loved me, parents who wanted the best for me and a few friends at school as well. Plus, my grades started to improve and I eventually got into that prestigious school I'd been striving towards.

Even at that young age I remember thinking that getting into that school would enable me to get better grades, and this in turn would allow me to get into a top university and then to find a fantastic job. Life looked so linear and planned out. I was already under the impression that these goals were at least in part what contributed to personal happiness.

I sometimes wonder: what if I had realised back then that I didn't need to strive so hard? What if someone had pointed me to the possibility that I could do whatever I really wanted? I'm sure I'm not the only one who had some version of this growing up. Did you ever think that there was some goal that, once achieved, would make life complete for you?

Well, I'm still lucky I found this out for myself years later—but we'll get to that.

CHAPTER 3.

My Lowest Point
and a Glimmer of Hope

"Pthu!"

I was sitting at my desk, waiting for our teacher to walk in, when the spit flew from John's mouth and landed on my cheek.

John was, in my mind at least, one of the cool kids. He was a rugby player. He was popular and clever too.

I, on the other hand, was skinny, uncool and athletically challenged.

The desks all had various unintelligent graffiti etched into them as boys tried to leave their mark through the years. Light streamed in from the two large windows behind me. To the right, behind John and his friend Christopher, were rows of metal lockers where we kept our bags, books and gym equipment.

I wiped the spit off my face and just stared at my desk as John and Christopher watched me and laughed. In that moment, I felt so small, unworthy and unimportant. It didn't even occur to me to fight back, to say anything or even report him to the teacher. In fact, even our teacher seemed to adore John.

I had few friends, and even though I'd worked for years to get into this top school, my experience now didn't seem much better than when I'd been struggling to get in.

But it is often in our lowest moments that we find hope. For me that hope came in the form of a classmate—Kevin. A few days after the spitting incident I got into conversation with a Kevin and told him what had happened. Kevin said that if John had spat at him, he would have spit right back. This shocked me because Kevin was of a similar size and build to me.

"What if you get beaten up?" I asked him.

Kevin was unaffected. He had a confidence I admired, and he was kind too. For some reason, he took me under his wing, introduced me to his friends and helped to remind me that I didn't need to be so afraid of John. In fact, I didn't need to be so afraid of *life*.

It's amazing the impact a little kindness can have on someone's life. I felt like I had finally been given permission to be myself once more. For the remainder of the school year I started enjoying school and hanging around with my new friends.

I frequently tell my clients:

We often underestimate the impact we have on others

It's probably safe to say that neither John nor Kevin really knew at the time what was happening in my head and how I was feeling about their actions. However, that episode left its mark. I tried to be as kind to others as Kevin had been to me. Looking back now I have no ill will towards John, and he probably can't even remember the event. He was doing what made sense to him in that moment. I'm sure everyone reading this has done things in the past that in hindsight they wouldn't do now.

I feel that John and bullies like him are not bad people. They are acting and behaving based on what they think makes sense to them. For my own part, I know that I have been mean, selfish, unkind and judgmental towards others at times. Does this make me a bad person? I used to think so. However, I think it is a side effect of forgetting who we really are—of forgetting about that part of us of which we had greater understanding when we were children. Just like when I was a little boy, kindness has always been within me—just as it is within you.

Perhaps what bullies need is not to be shamed or given a taste of their own medicine, but a reminder of who they are.

CHAPTER 4.

An Introduction to Personal Development

I started my management degree at Aston University in Birmingham, England. Academically I found the first year quite easy. What I didn't find so easy were relationships with other people—specifically women. I had a belief at the time, one which lasted for a great many years, that I could only be truly happy once I had met my soulmate. I didn't think there was only one person out there who could be my soulmate but I did feel that until I met someone who fit the bill I would not be complete. I had totally forgotten the joy I felt as a child who held none of these thoughts.

I remember thinking that the reason we sometimes call our partner our "other half" is because we feel we are only one half of a whole. One side effect of this belief in my case was tremendous neediness and insecurity around women. This had the effect of either repelling women or putting me firmly in the "friend zone."

One day, a very good friend of mine called Abdul, decided to help me out.

"Do you promise not to tell anyone if I let you in on a secret?"

We were in the small bedroom of his student house in Birmingham. It was in a rundown part of the city but was an easy commute to the university. It was also cheap and hence had plenty of student accommodation. Abdul didn't have a girlfriend either, but he was certainly not as needy as I was when it came to the opposite sex, and I respected his opinion. He also was a keen martial artist and had a confidence that came from knowing he could defend himself.

"I promise," I said, wondering what on earth he might have to offer.

He shared a few online sites which were dedicated to dating advice. At first I thought some of the techniques they laid out were very manipulative. But I had nothing to lose, so I agreed to test some out.

The first was eye contact. I used to stare at my feet whenever walking through university on my own. I guess my body language gave away my insecurity. Well one day, based on what I learned on the dating sites, I tried to do something different. I lifted my head as I walked down a corridor and forced myself to keep my eyes staring straight ahead. A few girls were walking past in the opposite direction, and one of them smiled at me. My instinct was to turn away or look down, but I kept looking forward and found myself smiling back.

To some of you this may seem like an insignificant moment. But it was huge for me. I experienced an incredible feeling of elation. I had faced the world head on and survived. Not only that, but a girl had smiled at me! I couldn't believe it. More than anything, I saw that how I was at that moment—shy, insecure and fearful—didn't need to stop me from taking action. I saw hope.

Perhaps if I kept trying things out, despite my fear, I could change my personality?

Soon after I read something which focused the next decade of my life: in order to have a fantastic woman in my life, I needed to be an equally fantastic man. This made so much sense that I wondered why I hadn't realised it before.

So began my journey of self-improvement to try to make myself into a man worthy of a great woman. I had forgotten that I already had greatness inside of me (as does everyone else on this planet).

CHAPTER 5.

Looking for a Feeling
Through Alcohol and Partying

When I started studying at university, I didn't drink alcohol, and I was self-righteous about it. I had been brought up to believe that drinking alcohol was a sin.

Well, within six months of arriving at university I started drinking.

Why? Perhaps peer pressure. Perhaps I wanted to fit in or maybe I thought it would connect me with others. What I found while drinking is that many of my inhibitions fell away, which is to say I didn't get so caught up in my head and second guess myself.

It seemed that when I drank, I became more like the person I wanted to be: fun, carefree and confident. I wasn't as scared to talk to people and say what was on my mind. I'm pretty sure not everyone felt the same way and that there were more than a few times when I looked pretty foolish, but at least people laughed with me. And I felt like I was getting what I craved: connection with and approval from others.

Except even this feeling of connection was temporary. It only lasted a few hours, and then I had to contend with the hangover the next day. Most likely I'd also end up skipping my morning lectures (and sometimes my afternoon ones too). I told myself it wasn't that bad. This was what students did. In any case, I could always point out students who were worse than me. If I wasn't the worst, then it was okay.

It also never occurred to me that I could have the same feelings while sober that I had while drinking and partying. In fact, it didn't even cross my mind that I could enjoy life without worrying about what others thought unless I had a drink. It took me many years to realise that approval from others wasn't something worth craving. There were always going to be people who liked me and people who didn't. The idea that I could feel better if people approved of me or liked me led me to engage in needy, approval-seeking behaviour for years—not seeing that I could like myself first and foremost.

My drinking was the start of a slippery slope.

One evening during my placement year at university (a year spent in industry between the second and final academic years) I came home drunk. It was the week before Christmas and there had been a lot of going on. I sat on my single bed in my small bedsit, listening to the distant noise of traffic. Apart from that it was quiet. My head felt fuzzy and I had an uncomfortable, dull pain in my chest. It suddenly occurred to me that I had been out drinking six of the previous seven nights, and on five of those I had been drunk. I knew this wasn't healthy behaviour, and in that moment I made a decision to change. I decided to stop drinking from that day until the end of February the following year, just to prove that I could do it.

It seemed like a good idea. I was in control of alcohol and not the other way round.

How many other times in my life had I temporarily stopped an addictive behaviour to provide the illusion of control? Would I do it again? I convinced myself that if I stopped drinking for a whole two months then I didn't have a problem; I would prove I had the willpower to keep from turning into an alcoholic.

I lay down and drifted off to sleep.

After two months of abstinence, I went back to social drinking. Stopping without a deeper realisation about *why* I was drinking in the first place didn't address the root cause of my drinking. It would be many more years before something shifted inside me that led not only to a drastic reduction in alcohol consumption but also to changes in many other habits.

CHAPTER 6.

The Start of a New Career

I spent my twenties in what is called the self-development or self-help world. I read books on fear, influencing others and spirituality. While driving I constantly listened to non-fiction audiobooks rather than music. I travelled to Europe and the USA to take courses with world renowned teachers or gurus. I tried to stay in shape by going to the gym and worked to maintain good posture by doing the Alexander Technique (used by many actors). I even hired an image consultant from New York to help me dress better and appear more confident and attractive. I was obsessed with trying to be my best self, a need driven by a misunderstanding that the person I already was wasn't enough.

Not surprisingly, I still hadn't found what I was really looking for. All I knew was that I wanted to feel *okay*. In fleeting moments I understood this, but usually my mind was so busy thinking and analysing that I couldn't recall the child I used to be and how life was once so easy. So I committed to my strategy of self-improvement.

On some level it appeared to be working. I was gaining confidence and self-esteem, and overall I seemed to have a happier existence.

In 2012, after over a decade of this personal development training, reading, searching and exploration, I finally thought I'd done enough work. After years of seeking, I arrived at a place where I felt okay.

Little did I know that this was really just the start of one of the biggest phases of personal growth in my life. Everything I had known up to this point was just the tip of the iceberg.

That was the year I turned thirty. It seemed a big milestone. I thought I was old enough and experienced enough to properly be considered an adult, and yet I felt young enough to do almost anything I wanted. I considered a career change. I had, until then, been working in a large construction and building materials company that I had joined as a graduate seven years earlier. While I enjoyed my job, mostly liked my colleagues and had good career prospects, I knew deep down it wasn't what I really wanted to do. I asked myself, would my younger self dream of living the life I was living? I knew the answer was an emphatic NO.

I set one weekend aside to really THINK. I thought this focused attention would give me the answer I was looking for. So for one entire weekend, all I did was think about career options, what my hobbies were, what I enjoyed doing, and so on. I left no stone unturned.

As Sunday evening approached it dawned on me that I was no closer to working out what I really wanted to do. The more I thought, the more confused I got. I just seemed to be thinking myself in circles.

When Monday morning rolled around I set out on my usual drive to work. As I turned into the road where our head office was located, I felt pretty low, but I also realised I was no worse off than I had been on Friday. I then quickly forgot about the weekend's exercise and went about my day.

That evening, I cooked myself some vegetarian fajitas in my parent's kitchen. I didn't cook often, but I was trying to be healthy and this was a simple meal. The pan was on the stove, I had my wooden spoon in my hand and soft tortillas at the ready. With nothing else on my mind, it suddenly hit me:

"Why don't you coach?"

This didn't seem like a crazy idea. I realised that I really enjoyed self-development and spirituality. I also enjoyed sharing what I knew with others. I was aware that there was such a profession and that some people were earning a living from it. And it sounded like fun. I admit I was a little scared. I asked a couple of my best friends (who thought quite differently from each other) whether they could see me coaching for a living and they both said yes. I knew that I had to take the next step or I'd end up regretting it.

I enrolled in a one-year coach-training program with a trainer called Jamie Smart. It wasn't what I expected. I arrived on the first day of the program at a large, four-star hotel near Heathrow Airport in West London. Everyone seemed really happy—almost too happy. I thought I was in the wrong place. I was expecting to see serious, professional high achievers who were there learning to help other serious, high-achieving types of people. The trainer at the front of the room for the first weekend was world-renowned sports coach Garret Kramer. Now *he* had an impressive resume: he was a published author and had worked with Olympic athletes, pro golfers and NFL players. However, I struggled to buy into what he told the group. As an intelligent person, I thought it was my job to challenge him and not take what he said at face value.

By the end of the first day, I felt that I hadn't really learned anything. Garret was pointing out that our feelings served as indicators of our state of mind, and that our state of mind in turn impacted our performance. I found this and other material overly simplistic and I challenged many things Garret shared with the group. Surely our state of mind was only a small part of performance? Even if it were the key determinant of performance, I felt it would take years of deep work or daily meditation to master it.

Garret suggested otherwise. Years earlier, his own mentors had introduced him to important ideas that he had incorporated into his own coaching with elite athletes. The concepts were apparently having an incredible impact on their performance both on and off the field.

On the second day, after a nudge from Jamie, I decided to

open my mind and give the three-day workshop a chance. Doing so turned what I knew on its head and paved the way for many other insights—eventually leading to the remembering of who I truly am. For the first time, I opened up to the possibility that my feelings were a reflection of my thinking—nothing more and nothing less. When I was angry, my angry feeling wasn't telling me about what another person had done wrong, or how a particular situation had "made" me angry, or anything else. The feeling was simply a reflection of my *thinking* in that particular moment.

This blew me away. I'd never considered that anger was solely generated inside my own mind, that it had nothing to do with anyone or anything else. My feelings of anger always seemed to be telling me what an idiot someone *else* was—how wrong they were and how right I was. However, as I explored my feelings, specifically anger, I realised that I'd never known anyone who'd gotten smarter as they'd gotten angrier.

This insight was about to have a huge impact on all areas of my life.

CHAPTER 7.

Insights Around Time Management

After my first insights around anger, my life started to change quite dramatically. But one area where I hadn't expected these insights to impact me immediately was in my struggles with time management at work. I was a manager within the Procurement Department (sometimes called Purchasing) of a large construction and building materials company. I had joined the company several years earlier, fresh from graduating university, and had had several different roles within the company and was highly thought of. Yet my poor time management had hindered my effectiveness.

I had already spent some time trying to get to grips with time management, but I had made only marginal improvements. Being better at managing priorities had been part of my personal development plan, which was used to address my areas of weakness or opportunities for growth in my job. In addition to training delivered at my workplace and some mentoring from my line manager, I continued to delve into the self-development world through reading books and listening to audios, trying to get a handle on this problem.

Through all this I learned techniques to better prioritise my work, and putting these into action led to some improvements in my performance. For example, I didn't let tasks build up as much as I used to. Having said that, I don't think anyone would have said time management was a strong point of mine. I also didn't see there was anything that could make a big shift in this area for me. I believed anything else I could learn would deliver marginal gains at best.

What surprised me, then, was that after learning a little bit about how my mind worked, I *did* notice huge shifts in my effectiveness at work. I started to be incredibly productive. Looking back, I don't put this down to a technique or a tool I learned, but rather to dropping some misunderstandings I had about the mind which had led me to be very unproductive.

I'll give you a typical example. I would be sitting at my desk doing some work, when *ping*, an email would come in which would result in my becoming very upset or agitated at the person who had sent it. I'd feel the anger rising in my body and I'd normally say some expletives out loud. This would catch the attention of my colleague, who would enquire what I was upset about. We would then trade stories of how a person or group of people were stupid or purposefully obstructive and how they made our jobs more difficult than they needed to be. This often went on for some time and increased my agitation—as well as my colleague's. I'd then typically walk to the drinks machine as I felt like I needed a break, and on the way back to my desk I would walk into my manager's office. I'd complain to him and then he would get sucked into my story and also get upset. I'm sure there were times when it would be an hour or more before I was back at my desk doing productive work.

The day after I returned from my first coach training, things were different. I was sitting at my desk working on some document. Then *ping*—an email arrived in my inbox. I read it and started to feel angry and pushed myself away from the desk. I was about to utter some expletives out loud, when I suddenly caught myself.

What if my angry feelings weren't telling me how much of an idiot the person sending the email was? What if the angry feelings weren't telling me how justified I was in sending back a short, sharp response? Could it be possible that I was simply not thinking clearly in that moment? My colleague asked me if I was okay, and I quietly said, "Yes," as I sat still. Within thirty seconds the anger simply vanished and I was able to coherently and calmly reply to the email. I didn't pull my colleague or boss into a discussion about it. I didn't waste time going to the drinks machine. Instead, I found myself getting back to productive work in a matter of minutes.

As I stopped getting sidetracked by emails which I thought were causing me to feel angry, I started getting more time back in my day. What a gift!

My reaction to emails wasn't the only thing that changed. The way I approached my to-do list also changed. I stopped deciding on what action to take based on my feeling about each action. Previously, if it looked like certain tasks would be more fun than others, I'd do those first. Or, if it looked as though certain tasks would be difficult or boring, I would constantly avoid them. This is despite my experience, which showed me that when I did those tasks I had assumed were difficult or boring, they were never that bad.

When I started to realise that I couldn't possibly know how I felt about conducting a task before I did it, I stopped using my feelings as a barometer for deciding which tasks to do. I simply started doing the ones that made sense to do first, which was a far better strategy for being more productive.

Within a couple of months I had crossed off everything on my to-do list, completed tasks way ahead of schedule and even started implementing (and adding to) new ideas that were on my "one day I'll get round to this" list that I never thought I would action. What a change—and one that has stuck with me ever since.

Do you also put off certain tasks because of how you think doing those tasks will make you feel? Do you spend time doing things that look like they will be more fun, or at least less boring, than what you need to be getting on with?

Imagine if that was all a big misunderstanding and increased productivity and effectiveness in your work was just a thought away!

CHAPTER 8.

Anger and Road Rage

Several years ago, when my younger brother and I still lived together, we also worked at the same company. It made sense therefore to share a car on the way to work. We took turns driving. Despite this being a short, thirty-minute commute, there were often times where we could get angry because another driver had driven in a way that one of us thought was inappropriate or dangerous.

I'm not quite sure how this came about, but whenever the driver of our car would get angry, the passenger would say out loud, "Road rage 1", and it was understood that the idea of this quite silly game was to not stay angry. I don't know if it was male pride or ego but when we pointed out to each other that we had road rage, we didn't want to admit we had lost control. If we got angry again, the passenger would simply say, "Road rage 2."

To this day, I never remember having to say "Road rage 3" to my brother—or him having to say it to me. It's quite amusing when I examine it. Once my anger was pointed out to me, it simply dissipated. We all know that when we're getting angry at another driver, no matter how justified it looks, we aren't really acting from a place of clarity. There are studies showing that many people who act out in very aggressive ways while driving—"road rage"—are otherwise completely normal members of society without any "anger issues".

Does this mean that cars or other drivers have some hidden

powers to enrage us?

I would say "no", and as the rest of this book points out, the rage is coming from inside of us. More specifically it's coming from our thinking. Some days a car can drive very fast past us and we might barely notice. Other days it could infuriate us. The only thing that changes is our thinking about it.

Am I suggesting we try and control our thinking?

No.

Do we need to play the road rage game with ourselves or tell our passengers to do so?

Not at all.

Perhaps someone might invent a machine to shout out "Road rage 1!" when it detects our anger?

Thankfully, this is not needed either.

As I began to see more and more clearly the role played by my own thinking any time I was angry—whether when driving a car, at work, or in other situations—the less my anger seemed to control me. It was no longer happening *to* me and taking me along for the ride. Instead it was often a wakeup call to the fact that I had slipped out of thinking clearly.

There are some people who suggest that you *do* need to control your thinking. I tried that for a while and all it did was lead to more thinking and overanalysing. Not fun and not very effective.

Some people would say you need a conscious practice such as meditation or breath work. If these work for you, great! I don't practice either, but I have found that when I am simply being aware of my thinking, anger does not control me anymore. What's more, I am also able to slip into a quieter mind, which allows me to make better decisions and have greater clarity in the moment.

I still get angry, but when I do, it does not last anywhere near as long as it used to, and all my relationships are much better for it, not to mention my stress levels!

Try this out for yourself. Next time you are feeling road rage or any other kind of anger, consider that the anger isn't telling you about the outer situation—for example, about the other driver, your boss or your spouse—but is instead just reflecting your own thinking in that moment, and that it is pointing out to you a lack of clarity.

CHAPTER 9.

Going Deeper

By the end of 2012, my life was starting to change rapidly and I thought I had quickly grasped everything there was to understand about this whole thought and feeling connection. I even started to coach a few people and help them have their own insights about their lives. In early 2013 I delivered a half-day workshop to my team at work on how to better deal with our stakeholders. I was pleasantly surprised when they told me that they felt everyone in the company should go through the workshop!

However, as I continued my journey, I didn't feel like I knew more and more. In fact, quite the opposite was true. I realised I knew less and less about how the mind really works, and at the same time I was having increasingly deeper insights about my life that resulted in positive changes that amazed me.

One of the things I hadn't seen straight away was that I had misunderstandings about *all* feelings—not just the negative ones. My first insights were around anger, but I quickly began to see that these same insights also applied to sadness, fear and insecurity. None of these feelings were telling me about anything except my thinking in the moment.

What took longer to sink in was how this related as well to what I saw as positive feelings. Were my feelings of joy, happiness, confidence also only a reflection of my thinking in the moment?

I decided to explore this for myself and not take anything on faith.

I slowly realised that thinking my good feelings came from *outside* of me had led to disappointment in the past. One of the ways I realised this was in thinking about money. I had so many misunderstandings around money—the supposed ability of money or the things it could buy me to make me feel good or bad.

Let me tell you a story of where I thought money could buy me happiness. In 2011, I purchased an Apple iMac desktop computer with my annual bonus money. It was the most money I'd ever spent on a single purchase. I felt that I deserved this extravagant gift to myself because I had worked so hard that year. I was so excited when I ordered it, and was full of anticipation for the two days it would take for it to be delivered.

On the day it arrived, I carefully brought the large package upstairs to my small bedroom and placed it on the floor in front of my desk. I stood there, alone, staring down at it. Even the box seemed futuristic: the bottom was wider than the top, and its bright white colour contrasted sharply with the old maroon carpet it rested upon. That box was clearly the most modern thing in my bedroom. The carpet had been around for over two decades, and this was the same small bedroom I had slept in and done my homework in since I had been six years old. The desk was nearly as old as me. It was cluttered with books, stationery and my stereo, but a space was vacant for the new, shiny and very expensive Apple desktop computer to take pride of place. Feeling like a child on Christmas morning, I opened the box and unpacked the computer.

While it had a huge, twenty-seven inch screen, and therefore took up a lot of space, I made it fit on the desk, grinning the whole time. It started up quickly, much more so than my old PC, and came to life. I started to play around with it, excited by the speed, the colours, the look and feel.

But after a few minutes it suddenly dawned on me that I could do pretty much exactly the same things on this computer that I'd been doing on my previous one. Sure, this one looked nicer and was faster, but how big of a difference was that really?

My heart sank as I realised I had spent a lot of money on an object hoping it would make me feel better, happier, "enough"— only to find that these feelings didn't last long at all!

How many times had I done something similar in the past? Like all those times I pestered my parents to buy me a gift from the theme park we were visiting. My parents, knowing I would soon bore of whatever I wanted to buy that day, were always reluctant, but I would sulk and moan and use every trick I could to get them to buy me that thing. Yes, I was a brat! Even then, I thought that certain objects could buy me a slice of happiness.

This was important to me, because for many years I wasn't happy inside. The young boy who shared his chocolates was soon forgotten, and misunderstandings took over. I would be jealous of my cousins, whose parents would buy them better gifts like the Sega Mega Drive or the Super Nintendo games console that I really wanted. As I got older it was the Apple iMac or the holiday to Vegas or the sports car.

When I was twenty-one years old I was completing a year in industry as part of my degree. I was earning a low salary. Every day I would walk past lovely houses, new apartments and beautiful cars. While walking home I would often fantasise about winning the lottery and imagine how I would spend the money. My imaginary shopping list involved one of those new apartments, a BMW, paying off my student loan and a nice long holiday. This fantasy was fuelled by a misunderstanding—that buying these things would somehow make me feel better than I was.

However, that is not the nature of feelings, or of happiness.

I know now that happiness cannot be bought, that it won't come through a shiny new computer or any other objects money can buy. Happiness is an inside job. I knew when I was a young boy that there is nothing I need to do in order to access that feeling. I was born, as all children are, happy-go-lucky. Sure I would cry or get upset from time to time, but I'd always come back to my natural state of happiness. But over the years this state was layered over with misunderstandings that made me forget this. Forget that I don't need "stuff" to make me happy.

This doesn't mean I don't buy new computers anymore. In fact, in 2017 I replaced my now aging Apple iMac with a newer model. This time I knew it would be faster than my previous model and that I could be more efficient in my work when using it, but my happiness and good feelings were not tied to it. I can enjoy using the computer as a wonderful tool for many tasks, including writing this book. But I no longer think that a new computer will make me feel happy.

Is this true of *all* feelings? What about romantic love?

Yes, this understanding applies here as well. For example, I see now how thinking that any of my good feelings come from my wife is a huge misunderstanding. In fact, knowing that my good or bad feelings have nothing to do with my wife is what gave me some certainty about the future when I proposed to her. I realised feelings change from time to time, and if I expected good feelings to come from her, then when it seemed as if they didn't (as I'm sure happens in all relationships at some point) our marriage might be on shaky ground. However, if I saw that my good or bad feelings were only a reflection of my thinking in any particular moment, then my marriage was more solid; it was based on a choice to be with my wife, regardless of my feelings in any given moment.

Over the last few years, I've come to see there are no exceptions to how our minds work. Now, you may think that this is a rather cold, unloving and boring way to live life, but my experience has not reflected this. I am completely in love with my wife, and if we disagree and argue because I have momentarily lost sight of where my feelings are coming from, I'm only one thought away from that loving feeling again. This has meant a much more fruitful, happy relationship, and one in which I keep learning and growing each day.

CHAPTER 10.

Is Forgiveness Really Necessary?

In 2011, I wrote the following status update on Facebook:

"As I lie down to sleep tonight, let it be in gratitude for my life and in forgiveness to anyone who has wronged me."

You may read that and think it is a noble sentiment. For many years I thought forgiveness was a sign of maturity or wisdom. It seemed difficult at times, but I thought that if I could forgive those who had wronged me, then there was nothing more to be done. Forgiveness was common sense, and it was also incorporated into many spiritual teachings. I didn't imagine there was anything deeper to uncover or learn about forgiveness.

However, in 2014 I was telling a mentor of mine (Dr. Keith Blevens—who is a pioneer in this understanding) that I felt I had made significant steps forward by learning to forgive certain people in my life. I was surprised when he asked me, "Why would you need to forgive someone?"

Needless to say, I was quite taken aback. I wasn't sure what to say. I was sitting on my large bed in my London apartment talking to him via Skype on one of our regular mentoring conversations. He then added, "You only need to forgive someone if they had the power to hurt you in the first place."

I felt my mind go very quiet and I sat very still. In that moment, everything I thought I knew about forgiveness was turned on its head and my brain felt like it was rebooting. The reason I was going through the process of forgiveness was to let go of angry and hurt feelings based on what other people had done. However, Dr. Blevens pointed out to me something I thought I already knew. My hurt or angry feelings weren't coming from other people at all. They were coming from my own *thinking* about what people had done or said. The actions of other people had nothing to do with how I *felt* about those actions, even though that is how it looked to me.

This understanding totally changed my relationship to the concept of forgiveness—I suddenly realised it was unnecessary, because if no-one could make me feel anything, then forgiveness no longer made any logical sense.

No matter how strange it looked to me, when other people took actions that I thought hurt my feelings, they were acting in ways that made complete sense to them at the time. For all I knew they may have felt as if they had no choice—if they had they would have likely behaved differently. But I interpreted their actions and behaviours through my own thinking, assigning a meaning that might have had nothing to do with what was actually going on inside their heads.

Just as my thinking is fleeting and can change in an instant, so too can feelings of hurt and anger.

I now believe that we do not need to forgive anyone in our lives for anything they have done—once we realise that what we *feel* about their actions is simply a reflection of our own *thinking* about their actions. Until we realise this it's as if we're giving other people the power to make us feel a certain way. Not only is this completely unnecessary, it can cause us to feel further resentment. But when we *do* realise that no one else has the power to make us feel a certain way, we can live a much happier life— without carrying around resentment like a backpack full of rocks.

A client[*] of mine had his own huge insight around

---

[*] I have changed names and identifying details throughout this book to protect privacy.

forgiveness. His father had passed away many years earlier and my client had a lot of resentment towards him for not being a better father. He had trouble forgiving him, and years after his father's death he still held a whole host of judgements against him. I run what I call "Immersion" events where I dive deep into what I am sharing in this book with a small group over a number of days. After attending an Immersion event I ran where I talked about my own experiences around forgiveness, he said he was finally able to let go of his resentment towards his father; he realised now that his father was human just like him, and that he had simply done the best that he could based on the thinking he had. As you can imagine, it felt like a huge weight was lifted off my client's shoulders.

I should make it clear that I am not saying that you should allow other people to treat you badly. Just as it doesn't make logical sense to me to forgive someone else, it similarly might not make logical sense to be friends with someone if they kept on stealing money from me. I don't need to get upset about the behaviour, and I can understand that the other person is acting in a way that makes sense to them—even if I can't understand it. Also, I can choose to not be friends with them.

What if we didn't need to forgive anyone who "hurts" us? I invite you to think of anyone against whom you hold any judgements or resentments. Ask yourself if these people really did hurt you or whether your hurt feelings are reflections of your own thinking about their actions. If so, what if you did not need to struggle to forgive them? What if this were completely unnecessary and you could simply drop any lingering hurt, anger or resentment?

CHAPTER 11.

Is Acceptance Necessary?

I used to think that "acceptance" was something I had to practice in order to move on with my life. Apparently, according to many spiritual teachers, my issues in life were caused by non-acceptance. Whatever happened, I had to learn to accept it before I could move past it. So I now had another thing to add to my to-do list in order to live a happy life. I had to accept the things I couldn't change!

And yet, here too I reached a point where I realised—just as I did with forgiveness—that if I am experiencing life through my own thinking, acceptance isn't necessary. For example, if I had to accept my parents as they were in order to be at peace with that relationship, it implied that my parents were in some way causing me to not feel at peace. Here again there seemed to be an underlying assumption that people or things had the power to make me feel bad, unhappy or upset, and the best I could do was accept things just as they were. Then, finally, I could move on, despite these other people or circumstances.

What if this is all backwards? What if nothing—whether it's my parents, boss, bank balance or something else—has the power to make me feel anything? If nothing can make me feel good or bad, then I bypass the need for acceptance.

Acceptance is only necessary if we give circumstances or other people the power to make us feel anything. Also, why is it that we only seem to need to accept things that are "bad"? We don't say that we need to accept we are falling in love. We don't say I need to accept this circumstance of going on holiday. I've never had to accept my happy, positive or joyful emotions.

Some people say we need to accept our negative feelings or we will end up repressing them. However, we only repress emotions and feelings if we think we shouldn't be having them. If we see that we don't get to control our thinking, that we don't choose what thoughts pop up in a split second, then we will feel a full range of emotions and there is nothing to do about it. Often trying to *do* something about a feeling we have *reinforces* it rather than allowing it to pass naturally.

Once I stopped trying to accept things I experienced a wonderful side effect: I saw circumstances and people in my life differently. I started to deeply appreciate my family and stopped trying to change or accept them. I started to see that the times where I was not thinking clearly were times when I contributed to a less-than-smooth relationship with other family members. I also saw that any negative feelings didn't "hang around" for as long as they used to. Prior to understanding about the thought-feeling connection, I would ruminate for days over something someone had said to me. I'd play out scenarios in my head of how I could have made a clever comeback. However, because I stopped trying to change my feelings, the negative feelings would often pass quite quickly.

I also started to see opportunities everywhere. For example, I realised I could have much deeper relationships with everyone in my life, even with people I had struggled to simply be around in the past.

Imagine how your life could shift if you didn't need to change or accept others in order to feel better. Imagine how your life could shift if you didn't need to change your circumstances in order to feel better. What if you didn't need to process or accept any negative feelings you were having?

Acceptance is another thing you can cross off your to-do list. Simply carry on and enjoy life.

CHAPTER 12.

My Feeling Guilty Was not Indicative of a Conscience

For many years I thought that feeling guilty meant I was a good person. I never questioned this connection at all. I thought that if I didn't feel guilty it meant I didn't have a conscience. And as I was brought up to be a good person I hadn't ever considered that guilt was simply a feeling, and that any meaning attached to it was made up.

One day I was reading a book by the late Dr. Wayne Dyer (*Your Erroneous Zones*) and I came to a section on guilt. Dyer's book helped me realise that feeling guilty didn't make me a good person—it just made me *think* I was a good person. But no matter what I thought, I wasn't helping anyone else in the world by feeling guilty. Instead I was just wallowing in this guilty feeling as a hapless victim.

I decided from that day onwards that whenever I felt guilty, I would do something positive about it rather than simply feel bad.

For example, for many years I felt guilty about not being a great brother. In particular I used to be mean to my youngest sibling and would beat him up for no reason. The pattern was that I would be bullied or have a tough time at school, I would feel bad, and when I got home I would take it out on him. As we grew older we didn't have a great relationship—and I felt really guilty about it. However, I never said anything directly to him about it, and my tentative attempts to reach out didn't go well. After reading *Your Erroneous Zones*, I made a conscious effort to shift that energy of feeling guilty towards building a better relationship with my brother.

However, it still looked to me as if my motivation to build a better relationship sprang from my feelings of guilt. While Dr. Dyer's book helped me to a certain extent, it looked like I was still playing a kind of game where I was a person of good moral character because I felt bad. It also didn't help me to see those feelings of guilt for what they really are—simply reflections of my thinking in the present moment.

What I now understand is that guilt simply cannot tell me whether I am a good person or a bad person. There is no chart on which I can check the amount of guilt I'm feeling and see how it corresponds to my "goodness" or otherwise. Guilt is a reflection of my thinking about a certain action or behaviour I have taken, or not taken, in the past. Guilt does not and cannot change the past. It often doesn't even stop a person from taking the same action again in similar circumstances.

Once I realised what the feeling of guilt really was, years of guilty thinking started to shift and fall away. My guilty thoughts and my beliefs around them were like shackles of thinking in my mind that had kept me trapped in a mental prison of my own making. Once I realised those guilty thoughts were just thoughts, the shackles opened. I was free.

I see now that far from making me a bad person, dropping my guilty thinking has allowed me to be much kinder to others, a more helpful member of society and ultimately a happier person too. What's more, as these beliefs around guilt disappeared, my relationship with my siblings markedly improved. I didn't need to be motivated by guilt in order to build a better relationship with them. I could do it simply because I wanted to. My guilty thinking had been clouding my mind for years and I'd never known any better; now I did.

I also don't need anyone else in the world to feel guilty for their behaviours or actions. I used to want a few people to feel bad for their actions. I thought it might make me feel better if they felt bad, or perhaps it would make it easier to forgive them. It simply does not make sense anymore. If someone *does* feel bad about their actions, they are also just feeling their thinking in that moment. As I mentioned earlier, forgiveness doesn't make sense when you understand that someone's actions can't make you feel anything. Similarly, someone feeling bad can't make me feel good or satisfied or content.

If you're wondering how to drop your guilty thinking, I advise the following: don't even try. Your guilty thinking is only held in place *by* your thinking. Not engaging with it, not analysing it, not *thinking* about it will allow it to pass right on by—as it was always meant to do. What a gift to give yourself.

CHAPTER 13.

Can Fear and Love Coexist?

For most of my life I lived in fear. I might not have described it this way, but it was my reality. I was scared of being beaten up in a fight, scared of getting bad grades at school, scared of being alone, scared of being hurt and scared of not living up to other people's expectations of me. This fear-based reality I lived in was absolutely real to me and it didn't seem like I could do anything about it. I truly believed my personality was fixed and that at best I could only make incremental changes in my life.

In 2015 my coach, Steve Chandler, pointed me to a distinction about fear versus love. After sharing with me some of his own fears he told me that we couldn't feel love and fear at the same time. This was a new idea to me, and I tested it in my own mind. Could fear and love coexist?

It occurred to me that whenever I wasn't being loving to another person, or to myself, there was some fearful thinking in my head that manifested in my behaviour. For example, when I used to go out to nightclubs as a student, I often had fearful thoughts about being beaten up. This fear may have stemmed from one of my first nights out. During my first week at university in Birmingham, a group of us first-year students went out to a "gig" which was badly organised. As it turned out, the evening ended with a big brawl outside the nightclub. In the commotion a friend of mine—who just happened to be standing in the wrong place at the wrong time—ended up getting punched. That left an impression on me. From then on when I went out, instead of loving the music and the dancing, I often felt fear. I was always looking out for the first sign of trouble.

And yet years later, this flipped around. I started to really enjoy going out every weekend. While I was loving it, there was no place for fear or fearful thoughts in my mind.

The more I reflected on this distinction, the sharper I saw it. If all of my thoughts had to be categorised as either fearful or loving, I could choose to align them with one or the other—fear or love. I also saw that anger stemmed from fear. For example, if I was angry at someone lying to me, I was afraid that their action was somehow diminishing me—and I was already afraid of not being enough. But when I reflected on what I now knew about thinking and feeling I realised I could either align my thoughts with love—or with insecurity and fear.

Steve shared an Emmet Fox quote with me: "If you could only love enough, you could be the most powerful person in the world."

I started to see that the more I pointed myself to love rather than fear, the more effectively I lived. Love, I knew, was a reflection of my thinking. It wasn't outside of me. It didn't rely on someone else approving of me or the size of my bank account. If I could allow myself to love my studies, my grades would be higher than when I was fearful of not doing well. The more I was afraid of getting hurt, the more cautious I was, and this impacted my ability to deepen my relationships with others. I know for a fact that when I try to live up to someone else's expectations I'm not as happy or productive as I can be. But when I follow what I love to do, I'm more productive, more effective and happier. Perhaps it's more accurate to say that the more I saw fear for what it was—a reflection of my thinking—the easier it was for my thinking to return to loving thoughts.

I see the implication of this distinction globally too. The same year that Steve taught me this distinction, I heard the news of one of the terrorist attacks in Paris. I was bombarded with all the subsequent posts on Facebook. The idea that fear and love are opposites and unable to coexist came back to me.

You may recall that terrorists had attacked various places across Paris and killed hundreds of innocent people. One post on Facebook shared how a woman was caught up in a concert hall where terrorists had opened fire. She survived, but what struck me was that as she lay there, thinking she was going to die, she thought about her loved ones and wished they knew how much she loved them. In that moment she had thought about love.

I pondered on this. The "terrorists" who commit these heinous acts want to spread fear, anger, hurt and suffering. They want others to be afraid. This is true for all terrorists in whatever part of the world they are operating. I used to feel powerless when I heard of atrocities committed by others. I used to think, "What can I do?" In the past I have felt angry, upset, confused and so on. And whenever there is a terrorist attack carried out, I see these same feelings in others via their posts on Facebook.

However, I have come to realise that no-one has the power to make me or anyone else feel fear, anger, hurt or pain. In fact, no-one else can make us feel anything, even if it sometimes looks that way. Some may say that the best thing to do is to cultivate love, kindness, generosity and forgiveness. But what if we didn't *need* to cultivate these feelings or behaviours? What if they emerged naturally when we weren't caught up in our fear-based thinking? Like the woman who was lying on the concert hall floor, or like when we're children and experience a natural joy in everything?

When all other thoughts leave us, we are left with love—even in the direst of circumstances.

There is power in love. We do not need to be victims of circumstance. We do not need to be afraid. We do not need to fear those who commit crimes or who dislike us.

We simply need to allow love to emerge. When we do this, we tap into our own source of unlimited power.

CHAPTER 14.

Comparison Is a Mind Virus

There was a young man with whom I went to university. I didn't know him very well and in truth I avoided him. He was a big guy, someone I saw as a thug who got into fights. He had a beautiful girlfriend who always seemed to be running around after him. I thought he was cocky, arrogant and vain. I remember thinking at the time that people like him wouldn't amount to anything—if they managed to graduate at all.

A few years later I bumped into this same man in a chance encounter in a pub in central London. I had popped in to use the toilet and on my way out I saw him talking to some people I assumed were his work colleagues. He was wearing a smart, dark suit and drinking from a traditional pint glass. I instantly recognised him, said hello and introduced myself. He didn't remember who I was. He told me he was working for a large and respected consultancy firm.

I immediately felt insecure. In my mind I started comparing myself to him. I told myself that I wasn't working in as prestigious a job or at as respected a company. I imagined that he probably earned a lot more money than me and that overall his life had turned out far better than mine.

I felt down. I felt upset. And part of me felt that life was unfair. It wasn't right that this guy who got into fights, treated his girlfriend badly, and who in general wasn't a very nice person should end up with a much better life than me.

Well, after some time I forgot about him. I gradually spent less and less time comparing myself to others and more time thinking about what I wanted to create in my own life. It wasn't this man's or anyone else's fault that my life turned out the way it had. I see now, too, that I made a lot of assumptions about what his life was really like. The truth is, I had only the tiniest of glimpses into how his life had turned out. For all I knew he was on the verge of being sacked or promoted. He could have been married or divorced. He could have been happy or suicidal.

I didn't know, and it really doesn't matter.

It's easy to make assumptions about people, especially on social media. We see a few photographs and some updates and we compare the few highlights we get with the worst impressions we have of our own lives.

The funny thing is that others have looked at my life for several years, compared themselves to me—and done exactly the same thing that I did with the guy from my own past. When they shared this with me, I wondered what they were seeing—because I didn't see it myself! They made up a story about my life that was different from my own story.

However someone else's life has turned out doesn't mean anything to me personally except what I make up about it. Even the facts of my *own* life mean nothing except for the story I choose to tell myself about them.

Comparison to others is like a mind virus that keeps us small our whole lives. It keeps us in a victim mindset, and through it we give away our power to things outside our control. We are victims of our own thinking. Living in that world isn't very fun, to put it lightly.

When I spend less time comparing myself to others, I start seeing my own strengths. My greatest power has always been in being myself. I care about others, and my friends tell me I have a huge heart. As my mind gets quieter and I stop comparing myself to others, I am able to see this for myself. And I have other strengths, too, which I would often overlook. I see this with my clients, who often downplay their strengths and overemphasise their weaknesses—especially when comparing themselves to others.

What does this have to do with you? Well, you don't need to trust me or believe me or have faith in what I say or what anyone else says. Go out and test it for yourself. Do you compare your life to someone else's "highlight reel" on social media? What if you were to drop your thoughts of comparison to others and just take steps towards whatever you want in life?

You have so much to gain!

CHAPTER 15.

You Don't Need to
Change Your Thinking

If you've read this far, you may find yourself thinking that my main message is "Just think positive" or "You need to change your thinking." But what I am really pointing to throughout this book is that thoughts occur to us all day, every day—there is no stopping them!—and these thoughts are experienced by us as our feelings or our feeling state. Most of us simply do not realise this process is what occurs and instead attribute our feelings to something other than our own thinking—such as our jobs, our relationships, and so on. It is this misunderstanding which is the cause of so many problems, issues and inefficiencies.

So once you realise that your feelings are a reflection of your thinking in the moment, you may naturally think, "Okay, so then I will change my thoughts." This is another common misunderstanding. We'll continue to explore these ideas throughout the book, but I want to make it clear at this point that there is nothing wrong with your thinking or the thoughts that you have, and you don't need to change them. In fact, thinking that you *do* have to stop or change your thinking is a misunderstanding that can keep you trapped in an endless cycle of repetitive thoughts.

If for example, you believe there is something wrong with your thinking that leads you to eat sugary foods, you might try to stop thinking about sugary foods. In doing this you are in fact making it more likely that you'll have sugary foods on your mind. Trying to stop thinking about something doesn't seem to be a successful strategy. It's a little like when someone tells you not to think about a pink hippopotamus and then that's all you can think of. To try and stop thinking about something just involves more thinking and is what often gets us confused and feeling stuck.

Our thinking is not a fixed entity, and therefore it makes no sense to try to change it. When we do, we often hold on to repetitive thoughts and keep ourselves stuck. But when we let go of any misunderstandings we may have, this gives rise to *new* thinking and *new* ideas; it unleashes creativity and helps us have a better experience of life.

Now, you may have certain thoughts in your head that you perceive as bad or wrong or even sinful. Perhaps you were brought up to think good thoughts (as I was) but you may or may not be aware that it is incredibly difficult (if not impossible) to control your thinking. Does it make sense to judge yourself for thoughts you have that you cannot control? Also does it make sense to feel bad or guilty about so called wrong thoughts, if you cannot control these thoughts arising?

I am not saying you should listen to or act on those thoughts. We have thoughts all day that we don't act on because we know that it doesn't make sense to. If you have the thought of punching your neighbour over his blocking your driveway, you probably know that isn't the best course of action. Any thought you have that you don't act on doesn't cause any harm. Therefore, you don't need to judge yourself for any of your thoughts; you can let them pass.

Again, once you see this it doesn't make any sense to try and change your thinking.

Realising this was revolutionary for me. It got me back in touch with who I already was: the confident young boy sharing his sweets. It was only misunderstandings that I had picked up along the years that had led me to forget who I was; these misunderstanding led to insecurities, doubt, judgement and fears. These started to fall away as my misunderstandings fell away. As a child I did not label or judge my thinking and so did not try and change it. I'm guessing that when you were a small child, the same was true for you.

In this book I hope to help you bring your own misunderstandings to light and expose them for what they really are: FALSE. In doing so you will start to experience your true self more easily and enjoy the feeling of wellbeing that is always present, even when it might not feel like it is.

CHAPTER 16.

The Feeling of Love for Your Spouse

I've never met anyone who at their core didn't want a deep, loving relationship with their spouse. But I knew of very few examples where people who had been together for a long time still seemed as in love with each other as when they had first met. In fact, the phenomenon seemed to be so rare that I doubted whether it was possible for the vast majority of people to keep those loving feelings alive over a long-term relationship.

But as the years passed and I deepened my understanding of the inside-out nature of our reality, I met a number of couples who had been together for decades and who were still deeply in love. In fact, many of them told me they were more in love than they had ever been, and it showed.

How could this be?

One night when I was away from home running an Immersion event for men, I lay in my hotel bed thinking about my wife. I smiled as I recalled how beautiful she looked on our wedding day. I felt so much love for her that day. Then I remembered back to a year earlier, when one evening, again lying on my hotel bed during another Immersion event, I decided I was going to propose to her. I started scheming and planning about how to make the proposal absolutely perfect. Once again, I felt the loving feelings I had felt for my wife during that time.

At the time of writing, my wife and I have not been married all that long—just a couple of years. From time to time, once we started living together (which we only did after we got married), we have had some small disagreements. These tended to be over really small, mundane stuff, which friends and family told me was completely normal when two people first move in together. Which way should we stack the plates on the drying rack? How much can we load into the washing machine? We were still very much in love with each other, but I would be lying if I said I felt the same way each day as I did on our wedding day.

Now as I was lying in my hotel bed that night in Birmingham, what occurred to me was that the memories which seemed to be generating those loving feelings were happening right in that moment. The feelings were *real* in that moment. I didn't need to think back to last year or to our wedding day to feel loved up. I could be loved up at any moment with her. A huge smile spread across my face as I realised this, and a feeling of love filled my whole body.

The next day when we spoke, I stayed in that loving feeling, and the conversation simply became an incredibly loving one. I couldn't wait to see her once I was back home, and the feeling was reciprocated. It was so incredibly simple to have the loving relationship that I wanted.

As an aside, I realise that amongst many men, it's not "cool" to talk about loving your wife. I often get the impression that men like to talk in terms of control. "My wife does this for me, she does that for me." We don't want to come across as "whipped" or "henpecked". However, I believe that deep down most men want to have deeply loving feelings for their partners, and they want these feelings to be reciprocated. In such situations, control is simply unnecessary.

I believe that men's desire for control often stems from insecurity about their spouse and a misunderstanding of the nature of loving feelings. If my wife is the *source* of my loving feelings, then it might make sense to control the relationship so I can ensure those loving feelings remain in my life. However, if I see that my loving feelings are a reflection of my own thinking about my wife, the control isn't necessary. What's more, seeing things this way is also a gift to your spouse—you are not putting any pressure for your own happiness on them. They can simply be, and you can appreciate them as they are.

Are you open to letting your feelings of love for your spouse (or your friends or parents for that matter) rise up right now, without trying to control them, without thinking about what annoys you or what you are upset about?

CHAPTER 17.

Gut Instincts and Insights

I had a belief when I was younger that I was a bad judge of character. I didn't think I could trust my gut instincts and I would be amazed at people who seemed to have this ability. It didn't make intellectual sense to me—how could someone rely on their gut to judge another person's character, and also have their assessments be fairly accurate?

Several people I knew relied on their gut to make decisions about their careers, relationships or other big life issues. Perhaps my reluctance to do this came down to not wanting to jump to conclusions about others. A very good friend of mine at university made snap judgements about others and felt very strongly about them, but I consciously tried not to do this. Or perhaps it was because I had some people whom I believed were friends and whom I later found out had lied to me or gossiped behind my back.

Or—and this seems most likely—perhaps I didn't feel comfortable relying on my gut because I would overthink things constantly. Whenever there was a decision to be made, I would ask a number of people who all had different ideas, and this would often leave my mind spinning.

In my twenties I spent time in the self-development community, taking in more and more information, concepts and ideas. This encouraged my overthinking habit and I was constantly analysing things, especially my interactions with other people. It was no wonder that I couldn't tap into my gut instincts or my intuition. I wasn't giving myself any mental space for those thoughts to come to the surface.

Over time, I did start to have a clearer head. I began to believe that my gut was something I could train or at least listen to more effectively. This came about as I learned to rely on myself to make my own decisions—without asking anyone and everyone for their opinions—and then seeing how these decisions often turned out well. One instance was when I accepted a six-month secondment at work to move to Glasgow. It meant staying several hundred miles from home (which I didn't want to do), but I knew it would also be an adventure. I started to see that rather than overthinking every decision, I could simply *decide* to make a decision—any decision. I would learn something whatever happened. Each time I did this it seemed that my ability to tap into my gut increased and my tendency to spend too long analysing diminished.

Later on, as I was introduced to the facts of how all human beings create their experience through their thinking, I started to drop a lot of my beliefs, ideas and concepts of life. I began to see more clearly that I couldn't make a bad decision because no outcome had the power to make me feel anything. This led to a much clearer mind—and a quieter one. I find now that from this quieter mind I can experience fresh new thoughts that are not from my intellect. I call these "insights" and I know that everyone on the planet has the ability to experience them. Many of my own insights make up the content of this book.

As strange as it may sound, I never really knew what an insight was before this. Even if I had known on some level, I hadn't been aware of experiencing one. I now see that an insight can come up at any moment of any day. In fact, throughout history there are examples of people having ideas or "eureka" moments when they weren't engaging their intellect to try and answer a particular problem. Most of us have had good ideas when in the shower or while driving; that is, when we weren't thinking about anything in particular.

I see that in the past I wasn't giving myself the best opportunity to experience insights or tap into my gut or intuition because of how busy my mind was. This busyness was in large part caused by not understanding how my mind actually works. As I started understanding this, my overthinking gradually dropped away. Now I can regularly tap into fresh new thoughts and ideas and trust my gut to make decisions.

To put all this together with a little example: If I believe my neighbour has the ability to make me feel irritated, one side effect of this misunderstanding will be that I spend more time thinking about my neighbour. This overthinking takes up my "head space" and interferes with my ability to quiet down and hear messages from my intuition. But if I realise that my neighbour cannot make me feel irritated, upset, happy or sad, then as a consequence I will have less thinking about her and be more open to new thoughts and ideas. And perhaps some of those insights will involve creating a better relationship with my neighbour. After all, an insight is just a thought I've not had before.

Over the past few years, I have made decisions regarding career, relationships and money that may have looked like bad moves to others. But because I listened to my gut, the opposite turned out to be true.

For example, when I decided to enrol in my first coach training—which cost me thousands of pounds—one of my colleagues at work was very wary and tried to talk me out of it. He thought I was signing up for something that would be a waste of money, but in fact it laid the groundwork for my profession.

When I quit my corporate job in 2014, more than a few of my colleagues couldn't understand why I would quit such a great job, with its high salary and great future prospects. However, in both these examples (and many more), trusting my gut paid off for me. My intellect is a wonderful thing and it is helpful, but I now see that there is another, deeper place of intelligence within me—and everyone else. Once we tap into it we can begin to transform our lives.

Have there been times when you've trusted your gut and it's paid off? Have there been times when you didn't pay attention to your intuition and things didn't go so well? Take a few moments to pause and consider these questions.

CHAPTER 18.

The Power of Silence

You could say that all the years during which I lived in insecurity, I was also living with a very noisy mind. You might even say I had a black belt in overthinking. If there were contests for such things, I'm sure I could have been a world champion at overthinking, overanalysing and just in general thinking about my thinking. I can't remember the number of times friends would say to me, "Ankush, you think too much."

But what could I do? It seemed like this was simply a part of my personality and there really wasn't anything I could do about it. I had tried meditating once or twice but whenever I sat down my mind just kept going and I never got the hang of it. I even started to read a book on meditation but wasn't focused enough to get past the first chapter. Not to mention that meditating felt like just one more thing to do at a time when I didn't feel particularly adept at doing all the other things I thought I was supposed to be doing.

When I started to see that I was creating my experience of life from the inside out, many of my misunderstandings and tendencies to overthink and overanalyse simply fell away.

A quick example of this. If someone said something which I felt was disrespectful, I would typically feel upset by it and then play out the scenario in my head over the coming days. I would fantasise about what a good comeback might have been in the moment, or what I would say to them next time. I remember a specific time when a cousin of mine made a passing comment about my hairstyle as she was leaving our house. I ruminated about this for days. I complained to my parents about how rude she was and felt even more upset when they downplayed her comment. This was all steeped in misunderstandings about being disrespected and what my upset feelings were telling me.

Spoiler alert: my feelings weren't telling me that my cousin was being disrespectful. The only way I could tell I was being disrespected was by *feeling* disrespected.

Now if that feeling was generated inside me, via my own thinking, then *no one* could make me feel disrespected. I was the *only one* who could do so by thinking "disrespected" thoughts. Once I realised this I could drop all that thinking about how to "get back" at my cousin, because she hadn't disrespected me in the first place. I could simply drop the entire incident and move on. The same reasoning holds true for any other time in which I feel disrespected.

When I learned to do this, my mind was a lot quieter and I found myself living a much happier life. It's pretty obvious when I think back to it. If my mind is busy thinking about things like how someone hurt or upset me and how I can protect myself or get back at them, I'm too busy in my head to enjoy the present moment. It was freeing not to have a noisy mind where I was always thinking about one thing or another. I hadn't even realised how noisy my mind was until it started to quiet down.

I now find myself returning to this space of silence more and more. I still don't meditate but I look to spend time in this meditative space. It's the space that I enjoy rather than the practice of meditation. Spending time in this silent space seems to result in the insights that I mentioned earlier, and in increased creativity and the ability to come up with solutions to any challenges I am facing. Once you experience this space of quiet, I guarantee you'll want to spend more time there.

(Note that I am not passing judgment on meditation or telling you whether or not to meditate. If a client asks me whether they should meditate, I tell them if it helps, then keep doing it.)

I can also tell immediately when I meet someone who doesn't spend much time in a quiet mind. Can't we all? There is usually a noticeable lack of presence and a sense that they're not quite listening.

I was recently working with a client who was burdened by his own thinking and had been for years. He prided himself on being someone with a high intellect, but he was also full of insecure and fearful thoughts. These led him to make some ineffective decisions and kept him from truly being happy.

After pointing him to how he was creating this reality, his beliefs around various issues started crumbling and he began to cry. Ironically, one of the things that shifted in him came about when he realised that for years he had been attending events and trainings, reading books and watching videos to finally feel okay inside. He had mistakenly thought that more information would finally give him the answer, yet trying to digest more and more information made his mind speed up more than ever.

I could relate to him. I had walked a similar path myself. It always looked like I needed more information, and silence didn't seem to provide a solution. It's important to realise that silence *isn't* the solution in and of itself. Discovering the silence within us is a side effect of dropping our ideas, beliefs and misunderstandings. You could say that we are living in silence, but our misunderstandings keep us from finding that space inside ourselves.

A few days later my client told me about how his mind had never been this quiet and how he knew deep down that his life would never be the same again. I knew he had really heard something. I also knew that the more he explored what I had pointed him to, the more his old thought patterns would begin to fall away and insights and new ideas would pop up—just as they had done for me.

Perhaps you'd like to close this book now and take a few

moments to see if you can notice this silence beneath all of your thinking, ideas, beliefs and stories.

CHAPTER *19.*

You Are Not Who You Think You Are

I used to think I was my personality. My identity was based on all of the thinking I was doing. If I had "good" thoughts, that made me a good person. If I had "bad" thoughts, that made me a bad person.

I desperately wanted to be a good person.

Deep down all I really wanted was simply to be happy and loved. Because of this I ended up spending a lot of my life pursuing things I thought would make me happy. What I didn't realise was that I was expending my energy on pursuits that wouldn't have the outcome I desired. I had forgotten that as a very young boy I was happy most of the time. I ignored the time my father told me that the proudest day of his life was the day I was born and instead still looked for ways to gain his approval. I saw the world through the lens of my own thinking—as we all do— and innocently looked in the wrong direction for my happiness.

What I was eventually opened up to was the realisation that I am in fact *not* my thinking. Thoughts occur to me constantly—but they are not who I am. As I have mentioned elsewhere in this book, I don't have a fixed personality, and neither do you. As I dropped this misunderstanding, my thinking stopped having such a hold on me. It was no longer imperative to have certain "good" thoughts, and I no longer needed to feel guilty about having "bad" thoughts.

There is an important thing to consider here: we don't get to choose our thinking. Sure, we can consciously think this or that thought, but in general most of our thoughts occur so quickly that we have no control over them. Have you ever tried to think "good" thoughts or any other types of thoughts over the course of a day— or even the course of a few hours? It's exhausting!

I remember listening to an old audio by Sydney Banks, a spiritual teacher, in which he said that having "bad" thoughts doesn't make you a bad person. When we have "bad" thoughts, we have a choice as to whether or not to act on them. And if we don't act on them, then there is no harm done.

As I heard these words, a lifetime of misunderstandings fell away. Suddenly I had a deeper sense of who I was—of the "me" before all my thinking. For years I thought that any "bad" thought I had made me a bad person who had to try to be good. Now I saw this wasn't true. I was like everyone else—I simply had all sorts of thoughts come through my head every day. As long as I didn't act on thinking that was harmful to me or to others, there was no harm done.

I recalled something that had happened when I was really young, something I had never shared with anyone else. I remembered sitting in my room crying over something trivial. In that moment, at that very young age, it occurred to me that if I chose to, I could separate out the *thinking* in my head from a different voice. There was *my* voice and then there was this constant *thinking*. I realised the two were very different, but no-one had ever explained this to me. I got very scared and shut down my awareness of this inner voice.

I look back now and realise that I was always aware of who I really was. I believe we all are on some level. There are always clues being given to us if only we'll pay attention to them. When I now speak with my clients—or in fact anyone—I can stand in absolute confidence that the person opposite me is incredibly powerful, resilient and good. Not because I know them but because I know it is true for every person on the planet. The person opposite me may not believe this themselves, but that is only because they have some misunderstanding about who they really are, just like I did.

More often than not, when I tell people what I see in them, they acknowledge it. I remember the first time I told a particular client of mine that he wasn't a bad person, that he was innocent because he had behaved in whatever way made sense to him based on the thinking he had at the time. Tears started running down his face because he knew what I was saying was true.

We are all complete, whole, good and everything we want to be. You don't need to believe your thinking that tells you otherwise. It's not who you really are. It's just thinking that you can dismiss, just like you've dismissed other thoughts your whole life. You are an inherently good person. I don't care what you've done in the past, what thoughts you've had or what anyone else has told you. You are not broken, bad, worthless or any other adjective you can make up. Who you really are is perfect, unshakable, complete and whole.

Ask yourself: What if I really knew this to be true?

Take your time.

CHAPTER 20.

Difficult People Don't Exist

What if there were no difficult people?

For most of my life, I saw some people as easy to deal with and others as more difficult. These perceptions were fixed in my mind. I felt that at best I could learn to deal with difficult people and try to manage my relationships with them. As I read more self-development books and educated myself on topics like influence and maintaining strong personal boundaries, I grew proud of being able to influence a great many people. I felt like I could get along with individuals with whom others really struggled. I regularly demonstrated this ability in my profession.

What I didn't realise was the role my own thinking played in my judgement of whether other people were easy or difficult to deal with. I saw their behaviour as if my perceptions were completely objective, and I didn't grasp that my opinion of them was highly subjective.

At one point, for example, I was having difficult interactions with my line manager (and boss); let's call him Eric. It seemed clear to me that the problem in my relationship with Eric came down to his behaviour; what I saw was that he was highly critical of my work and miserly with any praise. I nicknamed him Mr. Angry as he seemed to lose his temper easily. This in turn looked as if it was causing me to feel upset and demotivated.

Not only could I find many examples of his "poor" behaviour,

I could also find many people to agree with me that Eric shouldn't act as he did, and that his behaviour was the cause of our poor relationship. Most people could understand my feelings about Eric, given the situation. In other words, I had plenty of support for my perception.

But then one day it occurred to me that while most people thought Eric was difficult to deal with, there were others who probably *didn't* think so. For example, I doubted that Eric's spouse felt the same way as me, and I sensed his daughter adored him. I then thought of people closer to our shared work environment and realised that some of my colleagues thought the exact opposite of what I thought. In fact, I knew Eric was highly respected by some of the people in our group. Taking this line of thought a step further I reasoned it couldn't be that these colleagues were stupid and didn't really know what he was like, and that I was somehow seeing the "real" Eric while they were fooling themselves.

All of this led me to see that despite how sure I was that Eric was the cause of my lack of enthusiasm and other "negative" feelings at work, my perception was simply a perception. What I saw as aggressive, others probably saw as driven. As soon as I realised this, my relationship with Eric changed. It wasn't all clear sailing after that, but gradually my own behaviour shifted, simply because I no longer saw Eric as the cause of my negative feelings. I started to see how *I* could actually have been the difficult employee in the eyes of my manager, and I went about changing that.

Within weeks this work relationship completely reversed. Eric and I started to get on very well and he remarked there had been a step change in my performance. I started to see positive qualities in him that I had completely overlooked before and even opened myself to learning from him. We didn't become best friends but the change was remarkable.

I often tell this story to clients of mine who have a difficult relationship in their own life in order to point them to the possibility that what they see as 100 percent truth about the other person is simply their perception. What I have learned is that it is never personal; other people can only appear difficult if I think of them that way. I don't guarantee that other people will change if I start seeing them differently, but I have seen remarkable shifts in relationships when I pay attention to the role of my own thinking. This opens me up to being curious as to what I am not seeing about the other person and where I might be wrong—which only gives me a better chance to get along with them.

I'm sure that you can think of some people in your world who seem more difficult to get on with than others. I invite you to reflect on a difficult relationship and consider: are you judging this other individual as difficult because their behaviour looks like it causes you to feel upset, angry, hurt or sad? Could you open yourself up to thinking about this person differently?

CHAPTER *21.*

The Illogic of the Comfort Zone

If you've read even a handful of self-development books, you've probably read about the concept of your comfort zone. This, the idea goes, is the mental place you stay in to minimise any risk of feeling uncomfortable or scared. But it's also where you remain if you want to be mediocre or an underachiever. We are told that we need to step outside of our comfort zone in order to grow as an individual and be successful.

When I first came across this idea it seemed to make sense. And as I started doing things that looked scary to me I grew in confidence; they weren't so bad after all.

For example, many years ago I was at a team-building event where I faced a particular fear of mine: heights. It was the start of a week of activities that served as the culmination of my graduate program in a picturesque part of Northern England called the Lake District.

I found myself at the top of a wooden telegraph pole, holding on tightly to a metal grip, thirty feet off the ground. While I had on a harness and helmet, I still didn't feel safe. I was the fourth person to go, and so far everyone else had managed to make it up the pole, stand on top and jump forward—at which point the ropes and harness would support their weight.

After what felt like a very long time, and encouraged by shouts of support from below, I pulled myself up on top of the pole—which seemed to be swaying more than it should—and with shaky legs I jumped forward and was lowered to the ground by my colleagues. When I reached the ground, I felt ecstatic, and for the rest of the week I had an extra bounce in my step.

This and similar experiences made it seem like I had found the answer to confidence and self-belief. In fact, I got so hooked on the process of challenging my comfort zone that at one point I thought that if *anything* looked uncomfortable or scary I *had* to go and do it in order to grow. Of course, I didn't do everything; some things looked just too scary to do, such as bungee jumping or following in my brother's footsteps and taking up skydiving. But these elements of discomfort and fear were often the only criteria I used to determine whether or not I should engage in a given activity.

However, it often took considerable effort every time I stepped out of my comfort zone. It was like I was fighting against myself in order to grow as a person, as a man.

One thing that was never pointed out to me, however, was the logic of the comfort zone—or of my *illogic* in thinking that the only way to grow was to keep scaring myself into being a better human being.

If you stay in your comfort zone, you don't need to feel uncomfortable. Is that true? No one *wants* to feel uncomfortable, unhappy or in pain, so it makes sense that we would want to stay in our comfort zones if that guarantees we'll always feel comfortable. However, while that looked true for most of my life, I saw that there were times where I felt uncomfortable when I was not necessarily stepping out of my comfort zone and other times when I would do something that I thought would be scary, only to find it really fun.

Consider this: If our feelings of comfort or discomfort are simply reflections of our thinking in a given moment, then it makes sense that we could feel uncomfortable doing something we've done many times before, something we have complete proficiency at (such as a pop star getting a few nervous feelings before going out on stage). On the other hand, I sometimes suggest to coaching clients to do the one thing straight after our coaching call that they are putting off in their life, the one thing that they know will take them in the direction of whatever goal or project outcome we are working on. Even if this is a small, simple step, it can often seem like it takes my client out of their self-declared comfort zone. They may feel scared, apprehensive and a little anxious. But then I'll get a message from them telling me it was easy—or even that they found it exciting and couldn't believe they didn't do it earlier. In other words, often a step that seems threatening is no big deal.

It would also make sense that we might *not* feel uncomfortable when doing something new—our thinking might not *tell us* it's going to be scary, so we don't feel the fear. For example, for many people learning to drive the process can be a scary one—their heads are filled with thoughts of making mistakes and crashing the car. But for people who have never entertained thoughts about getting into an accident, far from being uncomfortable and afraid when starting to drive, they are charged with excitement.

What this means is that our comfort zone is simply made up. That is, we create our comfort zone from our own thinking rather than it being based in fact or reality. And if our comfort zone is made up, and anything and everything we do is separate from how we feel and think about a particular activity, then our logic of staying in the comfort zone no longer makes sense: it cannot guarantee a feeling of safety or comfort.

Having realised this, does it mean I'm suddenly confident to try anything? No. Certain actions still appear scary, intimidating or uncomfortable, but now I see those feelings as a reflection of the thinking I am having and the ideas they often evoke as simply mirages or illusions of my own creation. For example, if I get some anxious feelings before giving a talk to a new audience, I know that the feelings of anxiety are a reflection of my thinking in the moment. However, like a mirage, they look so real and seem to tell me that speaking to the audience is scary and/or dangerous.

This is just an illusion.

So now every time I take an action that makes me step outside of my so-called comfort zone, I realise I'm not expanding my comfort zone but am instead showing myself that it is all a mirage—all built on my own thoughts.

Like a man in a desert, I will see a mirage and get tricked by it. But when I walk towards it, it disappears—proving to myself it was all made up by me. This completely different understanding of the comfort zone helped me quit my job, talk to small and large groups, create videos on YouTube, start podcasts and do all sorts of things that looked scary at first (including writing and publishing a book). It became easier to do these things knowing that whatever I was thinking about them was all made up anyway.

What if the things you would love to do but are afraid to do were not really scary in and of themselves? Would that change things for you? What if you've just created a scary mirage of what it might feel like to give a speech in public, ask out that girl, travel on your own or apply for that job? Take a few moments to reflect on that.

CHAPTER 22

Are You the Average of the People You Hang Around With?

Here is something else that I learned from spending time in the self-development world: all of us are apparently the average of the five people we hang around with the most. If this is true, we should of course hang around with those who are "better" than us in areas where we want to improve. Their success would then somehow rub off onto us.

Now when I first heard this advice, I didn't pay too much attention to it, although it did make some sense to me at the time. I saw the value of engaging with successful people. I hired coaches, went on training courses and was always keen to learn and grow. All this had its advantages, but the main point of only hanging out with "successful" people never sat right with me. Why not? Because I didn't want to cut people out of my life simply because they would "bring my average down."

Now, being completely honest, I did stop hanging around with some people who were on a different trajectory from me at that time. For example, one friend constantly told little white lies to the point where I didn't know what was true and what was false. I might have stopped hanging out with him anyway. Other friends gradually became more distant; some I simply lost contact with. This is perfectly natural in the course of life.

Having acknowledged this, I will say that a peculiar thing has started happening over the past few years. I see now that the advice I was given all those years ago was actually backwards.

As I started to see that I was creating my own reality and gradually let go of my misunderstandings, wonderful things entered my life. I got a dream job in London. I got paid more money. I started my coaching business and I met my now wife.

But I never really paid much attention to the people I was hanging out with.

I now have wonderful people in my life with whom I am close. You could say I'm the average of the five people I hang around with, but I haven't made a conscious decision to have those exact people in my life. The people I am closest to are simply the ones with whom I spend the most time. We resonate with each other. And they became a part of my life as I lived more and more the kind of life I had always wanted—but had been afraid—to live.

Some people who are very close to me now have always been close to me. In fact, some of my best friends have become closer to me as they've seen the transformation I have gone through over the past few years. They tell me I'm still me, but more present, calm and a better listener. Others who were more like acquaintances have become much closer to me, and some people have become more distant. I don't know this to be a fact, but I feel that those who now feel distant just don't resonate with the journey I am on and how I live my life. A simple example is that I used to like partying every weekend, but even before I got married I just felt less drawn to that way of socialising. As a consequence, my "party" friends and I just naturally hung out less and less.

Then there are people whom I never knew existed a few years ago who are now very close to me. People I have met through my teachers, training courses or online communities. If several years ago, you had asked me to choose the people with whom I should surround myself, I might have picked some of those who are in my life today, but I certainly wouldn't have picked all of them. And I'm so glad of that, because I could not have predicted the future—how people shift and change, what challenges appear in life and which people would resonate the most with where I am in life today. If I had systematically chosen people around me in the hopes that doing so would lead me to success, I would have missed out on some incredible relationships with people I connect to today—not for what they can add to my life, but simply for who they are.

What's more, I believe that when we drop our misunderstandings about ourselves, we unconsciously give others around us permission to do the same for themselves. So as we step more powerfully into our own potential through dropping our false stories and beliefs, we find others around us doing the same thing in their own lives.

I am certainly not perfect, and neither is anyone else is in my life. I don't find it necessary to consciously pick and choose the people who are close to me. As I've said, this tends to happen naturally. There is no doing on my part. Once you drop your false beliefs, stories and misunderstandings, you will start to walk the path you've always wanted to walk. Some will walk beside you and others won't.

It's not your job to pick who accompanies you and who doesn't. All you need to do is just keep walking.

CHAPTER 23.

There Are No Exceptions

When I first got introduced to the understanding that I am sharing in this book, I wasn't convinced. I had come across many self-development models, and I approached everything with a healthy scepticism. This tactic had served me well in preceding years. It involved taking bits of techniques and ideas that worked for me and discarding the rest.

But regarding this new insight I was gaining, it surprised me that even though I didn't really believe what I was learning 100 percent, it started to impact me in very positive ways. The moment I glimpsed the fact that I create all my experiences through the power of my own thinking, my entire world began to change. I was no longer a victim of circumstance in a life that had the power to make me feel a certain way.

However, I still wasn't entirely convinced there were no exceptions to the rule that my feelings came from my thinking. I thought there had to be *something* that impacted my thinking or my feelings—whether it was a particular circumstance or someone's behaviour.

What I saw more and more deeply over a period of many months was that there are, in fact, no exceptions to this process. Your feelings always come from your thinking. I tested this concept over and over—often in ways described throughout this book—so that it gradually became not just some good idea that someone had shared with me but one that was deepened by my own experience. Every time something happened that appeared to cause my feelings to change, I realised it didn't work that way. If I felt angry about certain circumstances or someone's behaviour, when I stopped to really examine it, it became clear that the anger was a reflection of my thinking in the moment—not a reflection of something happening outside of me. The same held true for positive feelings. They didn't come from the new job, the pay rise, the relationship or anything else—regardless of how much it looked that way. They, too, came from my thoughts.

Realising that there were no exceptions became incredibly helpful to me in dealing with challenging people and circumstances . . . because it made me see *there are no challenging people or circumstances.* There is only my *thinking* about people or circumstances.

I don't ask anyone to believe me or to have faith that this is the way experience of life is created, but I do often ask clients to explore this understanding in their own minds. What would it mean for their current situation or problem if 100 percent of how they felt about it was generated by their own thinking?

When I ask myself that question (and I still do it often), it turns the problem on its head. I usually end up seeing I'm trying to fix a problem that never existed. Many times my only problem is that I'm feeling bad and I think it's because of something or someone outside of my control, so I try to change *that* rather than realising it is my thinking that is creating the feeling. A counter-intuitive implication of this is that there is often nothing to do. Our thinking changes naturally when we leave it alone. If our minds don't create feelings based on anything outside of us, then any problem is purely one of our own imagination.

CHAPTER 24.

Wisdom and Common Sense Are the Same

Why, you may ask, isn't common sense more common? We all know people close to us who have a particular problem. They can't see the solution to it but everyone around them can—because the solution is simply common sense. However, the person with the problem is so caught up in their thinking about the problem that they miss the answer entirely. This is their blind spot.

I am a perfect illustration. Not many years ago, the thought that I would one day be someone wise—someone other people would seek counsel from—would have been laughable. I spent so much time in my own head that I often missed simple solutions that were staring me in the face. I made mountains out of molehills. Everything was a bigger deal than it needed to be.

Could the wisdom that would have been so helpful to me—and which I am now sharing in this book—simply be based on good, old-fashioned common sense? I wouldn't have thought so then. Wisdom, in my mind, was something that came with age and experience, something that could only be imparted by an old man with a long, white beard, or an old lady who had travelled the world twice over and had twenty-seven grandchildren. I certainly would never have thought that I might one day be considered "wise."

But what if we are *all* wise beyond our years—just so busy

thinking, analysing and obsessing that we simply don't listen to that inner wisdom? As I started to really see my thinking for what it was—just thinking, and only what I chose to make of it—my mind started to settle. And as I have pointed out elsewhere, one side effect of really seeing how my mind worked was a *quieter* mind—one that allowed me to hear my own wisdom. The same holds true for you.

When I didn't know this, I did an awful lot of thinking about my thinking. I'd think about what I said, what I didn't say, what I should have said or done or thought. Once I truly saw that I am always thinking (and so is everyone else) and that the only meaning given to my thinking is by me—through more thinking— it no longer made sense to analyse or overthink. Once I saw that my feelings were not telling me about other people, situations or behaviours but were a reflection of my thinking in that moment, it no longer made sense to analyse or overthink.

If someone had told me this a few years ago, I might have seen the potential for truth in it, but it would have sounded far too simplistic. I also would have thought it could not be proven. At best it would have sounded like wishful thinking. I certainly wouldn't have thought I'd be writing a book about it in the future!

Now, after six years of seeing this in my own life, I *know* just how true it is. The more I understand it, the more I seem to align with common sense.

I can draw another example of this idea at work in my life from the time when I was debating whether or not to quit my corporate job and coach full-time. When I was making this decision, it seemed like a really big deal. I felt that the consequences were serious and I was constantly thinking about and analysing the problem, which didn't help. Eventually I decided to try my best to *not* engage my intellect and see what came to me.

Within a couple of days I was struck by the answer.

A friend of mine was offered a job by a coach. Although it wasn't a high-paying position, it would cover his expenses and give him great experience. It suddenly occurred to me that I would be at least as valuable to this coach and could do the same. But then I also realised that I didn't need another coach to hire me—I could get the same great experience working for myself while covering my own expenses. This had always been true, but my mind had been so busy I hadn't been able to see this for myself.

Wisdom shone through when I stopped overthinking. When I considered what it told me, everything made complete sense.

I like to think of wisdom and common sense as one and the same. For me, wisdom is pure simplicity. Once you hear it, it makes complete sense. And I know that you have access to your own wisdom this very second. This is because *wisdom is a universal resource that every human being has access to*. If your mind is quiet enough, you will hear it. I have seen enough clients realise and access this wisdom to know it is possible for anyone.

CHAPTER 25

You Always Have a Choice

Growing up I used to fantasise about being older so I wouldn't have people telling me what to do. I would finally be able do what I wanted.

(Well, that's what I told myself.)

Back then the choices I got were to clean my room or be punished. That didn't seem like much of a choice. Things felt out of my control, and most of the time choice seemed like an illusion.

As I got older, this situation didn't seem to change much. It seemed like I had choices, but again they didn't seem like real choices. For example, I could choose which university to go to, but I was expected to go to the best university I could feasibly get into. When I missed out on the qualifying grades to get into the university of my "choice" my father drove me up to meet the admissions tutor in Manchester. It wasn't my choice to go and meet him, and I felt resentful at having to spend half a day trying to convince someone that I was good enough to attend his university. He didn't agree (and I'm sure my attitude didn't help convince him either).

As I got older still, I started to feel responsibilities. There were my responsibilities in my job, my responsibilities as an older sibling, as a son, as a friend . . . I often felt that on one side was what I really *wanted* to do, and on the other was what I really *should* do. Yet all these things were wrapped up in the illusion of choice. I could either do what I wanted and be judged as selfish or do what I was supposed to—but didn't *want* to—do and be seen as responsible and mature.

No wonder I didn't have the best experience of life.

When I started to get a deeper understanding of my psychology, my concept of "choice" started to shift. I saw that if nothing I did had any power to make me feel a certain way, then my old way of thinking no longer made sense. The only reason I didn't want to spend an afternoon helping my father clear out rubbish and take it to the local tip (or recycling centre, as they are now called) was because it looked like that activity would be tedious and boring. It would make me feel less happy than doing something else. However, if the act of helping my father was neutral—that is, if it didn't have the power to make me feel one way or the other—then I really did have a choice. Or, should I say, I was able to choose without the misunderstanding of thinking that one choice would make me feel better than the other. I felt great freedom in this.

When I let go of thinking that I didn't really have any choices, I became far more helpful to people—not just my father but virtually everyone I met. Because now when I was faced with a choice, a real choice, it felt natural to help. Some may see this as me "growing up" or finally "maturing," but I understand it as a result of dropping misunderstandings and tapping back into what I've always known. Just like when I was a child sharing my sweets, when I drop my misunderstandings and overthinking, my natural tendency is to help, to share and to be kind.

It's been such a blessing to understand this as a newly married man. There are many things my wife would like to do that at first seem less than exciting. Grocery shopping, furniture shopping, painting the apartment and doing housework were never at the top of my to-do list for a weekend. However, knowing what I know now, it didn't take me long to realise that I can enjoy spending time with my wife doing *anything*. I also have a choice *not* to do a given activity, but now I no longer base that choice on the misunderstanding that doing something will make me feel bad, upset, frustrated or anything else.

Imagine how the world would change if we all understood just this one thing more clearly! What if the one thing you have been putting off had no power to make you feel bad, sad, bored or uncomfortable?

CHAPTER 26.

Why Is Making a Change So Difficult?

For many years, I knew what I wanted and what I had to do to achieve it—yet I struggled to achieve real, lasting change in many areas of my life. I would often initiate a change only to have it last a little while before I went back to my old habits. I thought my failure to change was due to the fact that my personality was a certain way. I figured it was harder for me to change than it was for others—or maybe anyone who could actually incorporate change into their lives was the exception that proved the rule.

It never occurred to me that my own misunderstandings could be stopping me from making positive changes in my life. What if my thoughts around the kinds of changes I wanted to make were getting in my way of making those changes?

For example, at one point I decided I wanted to stop eating junk food. Initially I relied on willpower to do so. However, I was afraid that as soon as my cravings for sweets and other junk kicked in, I'd feel dissatisfied with my healthier food. I believed my good feelings were coming from junk food, and my less satisfied feelings were coming from healthy food. This made it look like it would be quite an uphill battle to change that habit, one that would take a lot of willpower—and this was the main reason I resisted making the change for so long.

But as you may have noticed yourself if you've tried

something similar, I began to realise that when I ate healthier food I actually didn't feel less satisfied than when I was eating junk food. In fact, I started to feel like I had more energy than average. I saw that I had had misunderstandings about what cutting out junk food would mean for me. These misunderstandings were so strong that even though it was clear that eating healthier shouldn't make me feel worse or less satisfied, I still had this underlying belief. That made it hard for me to change my eating habits.

The same held true in many areas of my life, from money to relationships. When I had a misunderstanding about what making a change in an area of my life would do or how it would make me feel, my thoughts would set up roadblocks which I wasn't even aware of.

Of course, misunderstandings work both ways. If I believed that making a change would make me feel better, complete, whole, satisfied—then I would put an awful lot of pressure on myself to make that particular change. This in turn would make it far less likely that I would make the change actually happen. Even if the change wasn't a particularly complicated or challenging one, I made it more difficult by pressuring myself to do it. For example, I believed that by having a great, well-toned body, I would feel more confident and self-assured. I put a lot of pressure on myself a few years ago to achieve a certain physique, and I started training six days a week while eating six meals a day. This over-training led to me tearing my meniscus in my right knee.

Since opening up to how my mind actually works, I've made a number of big changes in my life. I found a job I'd thought was beyond me—and subsequently left it for something I enjoyed even more. I started my own successful coaching business, I created an incredible relationship and marriage and I've made healthier choices in my life and regularly work out. I've achieved these changes not by focusing on my behaviour and using willpower, but through a kind of natural ease and grace I would never have thought possible.

Now I'm not saying there was no effort involved. But it does seem like in the past I was driving through life with the handbrake on. When I finally released it—by releasing the misunderstandings I'd had about how difficult change would be—my ride became a lot smoother.

You may want to ask yourself: what areas of my life do I want to make a change in? What misunderstandings might I have that are stopping me from making that change?

CHAPTER 27.

The Real Cause of Complaining

I used to be world class at complaining, especially in work situations.

This was because I obviously knew better than everyone else. Complaining seemed like the only logical course of action when I was surrounded by people who couldn't see what I see.

Of course, complaining never really changed anything. And any pleasure I felt after getting things off my chest was momentary at best. At worst my complaining would send me into a downward spiral of negativity and overthinking.

On one level I knew that complaining wasn't really helpful and that it wouldn't change anything. But I also didn't consciously know what else to do. I had read books and attended courses which advised me to be positive, to look for opportunities instead of negatives. But whenever I found myself in a frustrating situation it was difficult to change my mind, and I usually defaulted to complaining to whoever would listen.

I never really slowed down to examine the real causes behind my complaining. If someone had suggested I do that, the answer would have seemed obvious to me at the time: the cause was the person or situation I was complaining about.

But if I had *really* tried to answer, perhaps even back then I would have known deep down that this wasn't 100 percent true. I remember complaining to a colleague about a line manager I once had. To my surprise, my colleague thought the line manager wasn't that bad. Of course, if the line manager was the cause of my complaining then surely everyone would see what I saw—*he* was the problem. But since this wasn't the case, I rationalised it that my colleague didn't report to this same line manager. However, after I changed jobs, the next person who worked for the same manager got on great with him.

Well, I thought, maybe people are subjective. They can treat everyone differently, so maybe there really was something about that line manager that made him challenging for me in particular. But what about circumstances? I remember once going through a period of organisational change. The company I worked for was undergoing a "reorganisation"—which meant that some people would lose their jobs. The first time I went through this I felt scared and insecure, and I complained about anything I could think of: not being given enough information, the process taking too long, the specific procedures, and so on.

A few years later, going through another reorganisation, I was *hoping* to be made redundant.

Same situation, different reactions to it.

I came to see that complaining is simply a result of misunderstanding—as are so many of the "problems" we deal with, and which I keep pointing to throughout this book. If I think that a line manager, reorganisation or the economy has the power to make me feel bad, then complaining seems justified. However, if my mind doesn't work that way then complaining makes little or no sense.

These days I see that I complain far less than I used to a few years ago. This hasn't been because of a conscious effort to stop complaining but simply through dropping my misunderstandings about how the mind works. Once I realise that the way I'm feeling is dependent on my own thinking, I am less inclined to look outside of myself for the source of any "problems" and instead look to change what's going on *inside* me. Complaining won't help that.

I still do complain from time to time, but again I see that there is never an exception to complaining being a result of a misunderstanding. If I truly see, in the moment, that my reality is created from thought and not by another person or outside circumstance, then complaining simply can't occur. It wouldn't make sense to complain. If the economy crashed, I could simply get on and deal with whatever I needed to deal with—without complaining. If my friend is acting in a certain way that I don't appreciate, I might complain. If on the other hand I see that how they are acting has no power to make me feel a certain way, I won't complain. I might talk to them about their behaviour; I might listen and be a great friend to them. I'd probably get curious about their behaviour. Complaining, however, would simply not make sense.

This is really helpful in my work with my coaching clients who may complain in our sessions about their spouse, their job or a politician. Knowing how the mind works, I can gently point them to the misunderstandings behind their complaining which allows fresh new thinking to arise for them. Often what they were complaining about becomes a non-issue or they see a very clear solution to whatever challenge they were facing.

Where are you complaining in your life, and is it possible that it's a result of a misunderstanding? How would it feel to let that go?

CHAPTER 28.

Beating Yourself Up

A favourite pastime of mine used to be beating myself up. (Figuratively speaking that is—as opposed to that famous scene from the film *Fight Club*, in which the protagonist *literally* beats himself up).

Why was I so hard on myself? Because I thought it was the logical thing to do. I believed that the only way to motivate myself to improve was to be tough and berate myself whenever I fell short of my own high standards.

This behaviour and negative self-talk was completely invisible to me. I didn't even notice how often I engaged in it. I wouldn't tell anyone because I believed that if they really knew how much I procrastinated, how imperfect I was, then the cat would be out of the bag and I would lose my job, my friends and any respect I might have had from those around me.

In my innocence, what I hadn't considered was how *nobody* behaves completely efficiently all the time. Nobody does exactly what they are "supposed" to do in exactly the way they're "supposed" to do it all the time.

If I stopped and really thought about this with a clear mind it was pretty obvious. When I look back at that time I see that most of the people I knew would not complete their to-do lists every single day. Most people I knew didn't prioritise effectively all of the time and didn't have perfect relationships. Most people I knew didn't eat completely healthily all the time. In fact in every area of life I could see that there was a full range of behaviours, and I didn't know *anyone* who was perfect across the board. I'm sure everyone was trying their best, but that "best" manifested across a wide spectrum of behaviour.

What I see now is that if I were to go about motivating a young child to do better in life, or encouraging someone who reported to me in a job to be more effective, it would make sense to be kind, patient and understanding with them. This would be the way to act with someone I was trying to get the best out of. Being really tough, getting upset and angry, withholding love—those behaviours would not only *not* be the most effective ways to motivate someone, they might be some of the worst. So why was I doing those things with myself?

It doesn't make sense, until we factor in the whole idea of misunderstanding once again.

If I think that I have to do "well" in life in order to feel happy, complete or accomplished, then it suddenly becomes really quite important to meet whatever goals I set myself. A by-product of this misunderstanding is stress—and stressful, "urgent" thinking—which leads to negative self-talk. I can't feel good about myself until I accomplish my goals, so I continue to berate myself until I achieve them (and then find new ones to chase after). However, if I can be okay with *whatever* results I achieve in life, or even feel wonderful, accomplished and happy wherever I happen to be in the moment, then there is no by-product of stress—and no need to engage in negative self-talk.

Now you may be thinking that this sounds like the road to mediocrity. I used to think the same thing until I tested it out. What happened was, as misunderstanding fell away, I became more gentle, loving and kind to myself.

And guess what?

The more gentle, loving and kind I was, the more effective I became in every area of my life. It surprised me at first because this was the complete opposite of the way that I had been living almost my entire life. I say "almost" because looking back to when I was that young boy sharing my sweets, I'm sure I didn't engage in negative self-talk—and I seemed to do pretty well back then. Many of my clients are incredibly tough on themselves when we start working together, but they eventually see that this is unnecessary and not the most effective way to live. Often for them it feels like a huge burden lifted off their shoulders when they realise they no longer need to be so hard on themselves.

What do *you* beat yourself up about? How does your own negative self-talk affect your ability to achieve your goals and feel good about yourself? Do you have any misunderstandings in this area, and what would happen if you released them?

CHAPTER 29

A Different Take on Procrastination

Another area I struggled with for many years was procrastination, and it's an area that many of my private coaching clients ask me about.

I recently worked with a client called Sarah (not her real name) who was struggling with what she termed "chronic" procrastination. No matter what she tried she always seemed to have difficulty getting done what she set out to do. I shared with her my own story about how I changed my relationship to time management, but she was still not doing the things she knew would move her business forward.

I could see she was an intelligent woman and that there didn't seem to be any physical reason stopping her from taking action in this area of her life. In fact, from the outside it appeared that she had accomplished a fair amount in her career to date. She asked me to help her get some clarity on why she wasn't taking more action.

I decided to brainstorm with her different actions she could take. I find that when someone is stuck, throwing around new ideas can be a good way to spark something that hasn't occurred to them yet. Half an hour into the conversation, she mentioned in passing something that she said she'd love to do, but which wasn't really related to the direction she wanted help in. However, she completely lit up when she spoke about this and clearly wouldn't need help in taking action in this area.

I slowed her down and got curious about this particular interest of hers. Our coaching conversation went in a different direction than the one we had started off in, but we let it happen. By the end of the call, Sarah was fired up about translating a book written in English into her native tongue. This wasn't at all on her radar at the start of the conversation, and it wasn't completely aligned to what she said she wanted originally, but the more we spoke about it the more she lit up and the more possibilities she saw.

It reminded me about my own procrastination around exercise. When I thought the only way forward was to hit the gym three times a week, I really struggled. I had tunnel vision—if I wanted to get in shape the *only way forward* was to go the gym three times a week.

Then I read a book on health and exercise and realised there were actually lots of activities I could do to get in better shape— from walking to yoga. I also thought that I had to motivate myself to exercise with no outside help. When my thinking changed, all of a sudden my problems with procrastination disappeared. I now have a personal trainer and really enjoy working out.

When we hold on to what we *think* is true, we can create a perfect problem for ourselves for which there is no solution. Then we wonder why we're stuck! Sometimes procrastination simply comes down to us thinking that doing a certain task is unpleasant, so we put it off. Sometimes procrastination appears because we really want to be doing something else and we're avoiding it for some reason. Either way, procrastination is rooted in misunderstanding, and once we sort out that misunderstanding we don't need to procrastinate any longer.

Sarah was held prisoner by her belief that her business could only grow through acquiring more clients. She was so convinced by this belief that she hadn't realised she could grow her business by doing what she loved: translations.

I believed I could only become healthier through weight

training at the gym on my own and so didn't realise what other options were open to me.

The fundamental misunderstanding that both Sarah and I were operating under was believing our thinking to be the absolute truth. But it isn't—and it can shift in an instant.

Now it's your turn. Pick an area in your life where you perceive yourself to be procrastinating. Is it possible that you have a blind spot in your thinking about the task at hand and that a mental shift could help you move forward?

CHAPTER 30.

The Real Source of Stress

So many books have been written about stress (just check Amazon) that you'd think we would have gotten a handle on it by now. Yet it seems to be an increasingly difficult problem for individuals and organisations. As I've pointed out throughout this book, for many years I believed that stress came about because of circumstances. This idea is reinforced in many ways throughout our society. For example, I once attended a training day in my corporate job where we were told to identify "sources" of stress, such as moving house, losing a spouse, debt or an excessive workload. What was not discussed was why—given the same set of circumstances—some people thrived and others crumbled.

I have a client called Ian (not his real name). Ian is a consultant who works on projects with challenging deadlines. Ian was extremely stressed in his job, so much so that even when he was away from work he wasn't really "present" with his wife or children. He felt his addictions to eating, smoking and computer games were a result of his stressful job and he couldn't see a way out of his situation, because his last job had had a similar effect on him; this was all he knew.

I asked Ian, "Do you feel this same way every day?"

He said, "Well, some days are worse than others."

"So you have bad days where you experience a lot of stress and anxiety and other days where you don't feel much stress at all?" He nodded. "Why do you think that is?"

He shrugged. "I don't know."

Perhaps he didn't have a ready answer because he had never stopped to really think about it. It only seems natural to think that our busy lives are the source of our stress. We reinforce this idea not only through our own thinking but in conversations with each other about how full our schedules are and all the things we have to do. So when I pointed out to Ian that he couldn't feel stress without some corresponding stressful thinking, he was sceptical.

I shared with him that the problem with believing stress is caused by something other than our thinking is that it leads us to think even more. This is what Ian was doing. When he believed his stressful feelings were coming from his deadlines, he started to think a lot about his deadlines—which in turn caused him to feel more stressed about his deadlines. It's a vicious cycle.

Over time Ian started to see the truth of this. Rather than being a victim of his circumstances he realised he actually had much more power over his schedule. Ian didn't realise that he was not alone and there was a whole team of people who could take on some of the workload he had. Once he did, he took his first holiday with his wife and told me that all the work got done while he was away. Previously he felt like his stressful thinking was telling him he couldn't leave work for even a day. This break helped Ian get even more clarity over his work schedule: he started to perform better at work, to plan ahead and take more time off. He found he was also more present with his wife, which improved his experience of his home life.

I can relate to Ian and my other clients who feel stressed out. I used to feel exactly the same way when it came to exams, deadlines at work and other circumstances in my life that I felt *caused* me to feel stress. The more I believed that, though, the more I thought about those circumstances and the more stressed I felt. When you feel stress is outside of you it's easier to feel you're a victim of it. It was only when I realised that my thinking created my stress that things changed. Without the excessive thinking I'd been doing, not only could I maintain my mental balance in what looked like challenging circumstances, but I could actually thrive. It was like having cheat codes in a computer game. I was no longer a victim of my own circumstances.

What types of circumstances in your own life currently look stressful to you? What if you realised they had no power to make you feel stressed? What would that do for your life?

CHAPTER 31

You Don't Need Motivation

I struggled with motivation (or so it seemed) for as long as I could remember. When it came time for homework or to study for exams, when I wanted to work out, cook, eat healthily or any of the many other things I was "supposed" to do, I gritted my teeth and sought motivation. And of course once I entered the corporate world, my to-do list was filled with things that I needed motivation to complete.

For a while it seemed as if I *needed* a certain amount of stress before I could complete these tasks. I would joke that if it weren't for the last minute, nothing would get done. Perhaps you can see a reflection of your own behaviour in mine.

All that time, what I never expected was to see that motivation is simply *not necessary* when we really understand our own psychology. If a client now asks me to help them get more motivated, I always ask them *why*. Almost every time they reply that they need motivation to get things done in their life. But this is simply a misunderstanding.

When I was very young I didn't need any motivation to learn to walk, talk or do any number of things that babies and young children learn to do. As I got older, I didn't need motivation to play computer games or attend my local youth group. Once in a job, there were certain tasks for which I needed no motivation at all.

I only seemed to need motivation when I had to do things I thought would be unpleasant to do. For example, if I needed motivation to go to the gym, it would be because some part of me believed doing so would be less fun than not going. However, any time I did go, I really enjoyed it. It was clearly a misunderstanding. When I started to see this everywhere in my life I gradually began doing things that I previously thought I wasn't motivated to do, like my bookkeeping or housework.

I recently worked with a coach—I'll call him David—who wanted me to help him grow his own coaching practice. David said that he knew what he needed to do but for some reason he wasn't doing it. It looked like a motivation problem to him.

I knew it wasn't a motivation problem—because it never is!— and so David and I started to brainstorm different ways he could grow his practice, just as I had done with Sarah (see the chapter on procrastination), who felt she was procrastinating about doing the things she felt she could do to grow her own business. Something similar happened in my conversation with David. We struck on a particular topic that changed the way he spoke: writing a book. He grew excited and enthused, and he completely lit up. We both realised that *this* was the direction he could go in to grow his business. In fact, we could throw out everything else we had discussed and just focus on this one avenue. His motivation problem disappeared, and ideas flowed out of him as to how his book could serve others and at the same time help him to grow his business.

Again, his misunderstanding had kept him believing that his business growth would *only* come from doing certain things like building a fancy website, doing Facebook ads, building an email list, creating a social media profile with lots of followers and cold-calling people—and he needed *motivating* to do them. Once this concept vanished a whole new world of possibility opened up.

If you think you have a motivation problem in any area of your life, is it possible that you just have some misunderstanding about the actions you think you need to take? What if any action you took had no impact on your feelings, either positive or negative? What would that change for you?

What would it allow you to *do*?

CHAPTER 32.

Your Thinking Isn't a Problem

I was speaking with a client recently, someone I'd been coaching for a few months. She was struggling with taking action on her business and she said, "I know it's my thinking—"

I interrupted her: "No, you don't. Actually, it's not your thinking that's the problem."

We touched on this topic in Chapter 15 but it's worth revisiting, because it's a common misperception. You may be thinking at this point: I thought it was *always* about my thinking! In fact, it might be tempting to read this book as all about positive thinking or changing your thoughts, but it is not what I am pointing to.

"It's not your thinking," I told my client, "but your *misunderstandings* that are the problem."

A light bulb went off in her head. She had been hearing me say that her feelings were a reflection of her thinking in the moment, and she had wrongly assumed that her thinking was to blame for her inaction. She thought that her thinking was causing her to feel lethargic or bored.

Thinking is never a problem. It just *is*. It's been said that we have something like 60,000 to 100,000 thoughts every day, and of those we are actually conscious of approximately 2,400. You've no doubt had many thoughts just in the past few minutes. Trying to control or change these thoughts is a Herculean task and one that doesn't seem to work too well in the long-term—at least it didn't work that well for me and it doesn't seem to work for my clients. Thankfully it's not our thinking that's the problem. It's just our misunderstandings—that is, what we think our feelings mean as opposed to realising they are just reflections of our thinking.

I'll give you an example. Let's say you're not taking action on your business or some other task you have got to do. It may sound like I'm saying the problem is the thinking that makes you feel lethargic and lazy. You may think you need to wait for your "bad" thinking to change into "good" thinking which makes you feel energised and driven. Have you ever tried waiting for that kind of change?

In my experience, this approach doesn't work well.

If on the other hand you realise that your feelings of lethargy and laziness aren't actually telling you that the task you need to complete is boring, difficult or uninspiring, then you won't be so tempted to put it off. Your feelings are only telling you about your *thinking* about doing the task.

This is true in any area of your life, as I have been pointing out throughout this book. We have all taken action at times when we didn't really feel like it—and things worked out fine. For example, we all know deep down that doing exercise will never be as bad as we think it will be when we don't want to do it. We know the rain doesn't really make us feel bad. These and countless other interpretations of our experience are simple misunderstandings. Feeling bad doesn't mean something is wrong with us or our lives. It also isn't a barometer for whether we should take action or not. At the risk of repeating myself too much I'll say again that our feelings are simply reflections of the mental activity in our heads in any given moment—and nothing more. Knowing this helps us drop our misunderstandings.

As I told my client, if your thoughts are the problem, then you are a victim of them and have no power. But if *misunderstandings* are your only issue, then this puts the power back into your court. As my coach, Steve Chandler, says, you move from victim to owner.

More about this in the next chapter.

CHAPTER 33.

Owner Versus Victim

As I mentioned in the last chapter, my coach, Steve Chandler, introduced me to a distinction that he calls "Owner versus Victim." He has shared this distinction in seminars across corporate America. In essence it is as follows.

There are two opposite ways of operating in the world. One is that of victim: things happen to you and you are helpless to do anything about them. Examples of this are where people complain about things—like their boss giving them too much work, the economy hurting their financial situation or their spouse nagging them—because they feel they are victims of other people or circumstances.

The other way to approach life is as an owner. When you are an owner you don't blame other people or circumstances but instead decide what you are going to do about the situation you're in or the goals you want to accomplish.

This distinction was very helpful for me in situations where I became aware that I'd fallen into a victim mindset; in such cases I would ask myself how to act as an owner instead.

What occurred to me was that being a victim was simply a result of misunderstanding how the mind works. If you think other people, circumstances or situations cause you to feel bad, then it is natural to feel like a victim. That's really the only logical conclusion of this line of thinking.

In fact, I would say it is *impossible* to be a victim unless you hold misunderstandings about how the world works. *Because if nothing outside of you has the power to make you feel anything in particular, how can you be a victim?*

On the flip side, I also realised I didn't have to *choose* to be an owner. Rather, being an owner was a side effect of having no misunderstandings about where our feelings come from.

A great example of this is from a client of mine whom I'll call Bryan. Bryan was a middle manager working for a large manufacturing company. He was constantly under pressure from his bosses, colleagues and even those who worked *for* him. He felt like a victim of his circumstances. Like his colleagues in similar positions, he came in early and always left late and still struggled to get everything done—he felt like there were simply not enough hours in the day.

Once Bryan started to see through his own misunderstandings about how the mind worked, he automatically stopped seeing himself as a victim at work. This didn't happen in our first conversation, but as soon as he saw his own misunderstandings they shifted instantly. No longer did he feel pulled in all directions. He saw he was far more capable than he had thought possible. Suddenly he was starting work on time—rather than two hours early—and finishing on time as well. This was while his colleagues still worked the longer hours he used to work. In addition, his performance dramatically increased to the point where he was achieving things that people had been telling him were impossible just a few months before—and he was having fun doing it. This in turn saved his employers a lot of money and he ended up getting promoted the following year with an increase in his salary.

We can all shift from being victims to owners, but rather than having to consciously choose in every area of our lives, the shift can arise as a natural consequence of understanding how our minds work.

CHAPTER 34.

Being Powerful from Within

In the summer of 2014 I started an online group called *The Powerful Men's Group*[†]. I was inspired by a coaching event I had attended to create a community where I could really help a particular group. It made sense to me to work with men who were from the traditional self-help world, which is how I would have identified myself. Looking back at my own past I realised that I had never really felt powerful before; I certainly don't think anyone would have described me as a powerful man. But I had come to realise that the true source of power doesn't come from money, a job title or anything else. True power is inside each and every one of us. I wanted to point others towards this realisation, to see the truth of it for themselves.

I began seeing remarkable shifts in the men who attended my live events for this community, which I called *Immersions*. Results varied from promotions and new jobs to healed marriages and new relationships. However, the source of this change was (and is) really inside each of these men. That power is always there. And it's within you as well. If only we all saw this more clearly, our lives would be truly different. This is why I've created events for women around this theme too. It's something that appeals to both genders—feeling powerful rather than powerless.

[†] If interested, you can learn more here:
https://www.facebook.com/groups/ThePMG/

So how do we tap into our own inner power?

Well, as I see it, I am not transforming my clients, but helping them instead to see past their blind spots. It's less about *accessing* our inner power than *realising* that we already are powerful. And we realise this once we drop our misunderstandings— transformation is then a natural by-product. Think of all the topics I have covered in this book, from stress to time management to relationships. Dropping misunderstandings allows us to perform better and unleash our true potential; the misunderstandings are standing in the way of our realising how powerful we truly are. Through my own experience and in my coaching work I've seen more and more clearly how virtually everyone I have come across has far more potential to create, be and do than they are currently utilising. I feel that deep down we all know this about ourselves, but we are so busy in our own heads that we just keep going. Our busy minds are fuelled by all the misunderstandings we have, and so it can already seem hard enough to manage to do what we are doing now.

I have a client, a very successful businesswoman in terms of wealth. But she feels her wealth isn't giving her the satisfaction she craves. In exploring this with her in a coaching conversation, it transpired that she really wanted to help others. She felt that no one had been there to help her when she was struggling, and she wanted to become the resource to others that she would have appreciated before she'd become financially successful. So what was holding her back from doing this? She offered several reasons at first, mostly involving cost, time, energy and maybe some training.

But as we explored this more deeply, she admitted it wasn't really any of these things. It may sound strange, but she was scared of succeeding. I was reminded of the Marianne Williamson poem called "Our Deepest Fear". The first few lines are:

Our deepest fear is not that we are inadequate.
Our deepest fear is that we are powerful beyond measure.

It is our light, not our darkness,
That most frightens us.

It can look scary to take steps towards what we would really like to be, do or create in the world. So scary that we can feel disconnected from what we are capable of. But if we see that fear as just a reflection of our thinking in the moment, it loses its power over us and falls away—and in its place we see how powerful we really are.

If no circumstances of your life were different but you stopped paying so much attention to your own fears, insecurities, doubts and anxieties, would your life be any different? Could it be said that you would show up more powerfully?

CHAPTER 35.

Fear Is not a Problem

In an earlier chapter I talked about fear as not being able to coexist with love. I now want to talk more deeply about fear because it can seem so real to so many people, including myself.

As strange as it may seem to say, fear is not a problem. It doesn't need to be overcome and there is nothing to do about it. Fear is simply a feeling based on our thinking in the moment we feel the fear. It's not telling us that we shouldn't continue doing what we are doing, that we are in danger or out of our depth.

Problems arise when we make decisions or take actions based on a misunderstanding of fear; for example, if we mollycoddle our kids out of the fear that they will get hurt. Let's say you hear that a child from a different school in another part of the country was injured on a school trip and you feel fear that you own child could get injured or hurt, so you don't give them permission to go on any school trips in the future, regardless of the type of trip or risk involved. The fear isn't telling you to protect your child by stopping them from attending a school trip based on a logical assessment of the risks; it's simply a reflection of your thinking in that moment. If you don't understand this, your behaviour may *seem* logical to you, but it also stops your child from experiencing a school trip that might have many educational and social benefits. When we see fear for what it is, our behaviour changes automatically.

The same is true if you have a fear of going for a promotion at work. The fear isn't telling you that you aren't good enough, that you shouldn't go for it or anything else. Once again, feelings of fear are only reflections of your thinking in that moment. That is all. Nothing more and nothing less. You can still assess whether it would be a good next step for you, what your chances are of getting the role and whether you want the job—independent of the fear. In fact, once you realise that the feeling of fear is just a reflection of your thinking, it often passes quite quickly. Once it does, you are left with a clearer mind—one that allows you to make a better judgement call. If you don't get the promotion or new job that you apply for, you can let any feelings pass (which is easier once you know they are just a reflection of your thinking) and then assess from a clearer head what your next steps can be. You might need more experience, you might need to prep better or you might simply just try again.

I often see where fear is holding clients back. They are confused, thinking that their fear is telling them who they are—but that couldn't be further from the truth. One client told me that he wouldn't volunteer for more work because he was scared of not doing a good job, even though he was more than qualified and taking on more work would have been good for his career. Once he started to get a better understanding about the role this fear was playing, he stopped keeping his head down and was the first one to take on more responsibility. He found he actually enjoyed his work more. He started to enjoy the challenge of this extra responsibility, which he hadn't thought was possible.

We talk about our fears and associate ourselves with them. I'm scared of spiders, I'm scared of heights, I'm scared of rollercoasters and so on. That is not who we are and those fears don't need to be permanent.

For example, I used to be really scared of rollercoasters. I never wanted to admit it to anyone else as I thought it would make me look weak, and I really cared how others perceived me. So, whenever I would visit a theme park, I would feel intense fear just standing in the queue waiting to board the ride. I would imagine falling out of the rollercoaster or the carriage coming off the tracks. Once the ride started, I wanted to get off as the fear reached a climax. Needless to say I was never injured and I enjoyed the rush of adrenaline once the ride got going. One day, realising that the fear was coming from inside me, I decided to climb into a rollercoaster and take the ride while staying completely present. I didn't pay too much attention to all the thoughts that were going through my mind in the queue or on the ride. While everyone around me was screaming, I experienced the rollercoaster completely differently: I enjoyed the speed and the rush, but I was no longer scared.

Now some of you may think that fears are good. Perhaps you're thinking you don't want to become a robot and that your fears somehow make you feel "alive."

I'm here to tell you that you couldn't become a robot, completely devoid of feelings, no matter how hard you tried. I still feel fear as well as every other emotion. In fact, it seems sometimes that I feel my feelings stronger now than before I was introduced to how my mind worked. Perhaps that's because now that I understand them as reflections of my thinking moment to moment, I'm not trying to suppress them. I know that they will pass as all feelings eventually do. So I'm not asking you to not feel the feelings you feel. I'm not saying that certain feelings are good and others are bad. I'm simply pointing you toward the fact that those feelings cannot tell you anything except the nature of your thinking in the moment. They cannot tell you about your self-worth, your confidence, what actions you should take or anything else.

Who would you be without your fears dictating your decisions and actions? I know that in my case I would be closer to that little boy in Chapter 1 who simply connected with others effortlessly. The boy who didn't have all that thinking about who he was, what he was capable of and who didn't need to try to be safe all the time.

Imagine how your life could change if you didn't take your fearful feelings so seriously. If you're inspired now, try it: take a look at one of your fears and see whether it could look different in the light of this new understanding.

CHAPTER 36.

You can Change Your Mind

Have you ever made your mind up about a person or a situation and refused to change it—even after realising you were wrong?

I confess I have done this more times that I care to admit. Too often in the past I made up my mind about something or someone and that was that. Even when it was obvious to me deep down that I could change my mind, I didn't want to "give in." I thought this would show weakness, and so I remained stubborn and rigid in my opinions.

I actually thought this was genetic. Someone once told me that men from the town my father was born in in Northern India were stubborn. By extension, I was too. I accepted this belief. So now, I had a perfect excuse. When I refused to change my mind I could say there was nothing I could do about it. That's just the way I was: once I made up my mind about things, nothing could change it.

It's actually amusing when I look back now. Such a simple misunderstanding caused me so many unnecessary problems! And the only person who couldn't see this was me. That is the definition of a blind spot—something which you cannot see clearly but which is obvious to others.

I have a client who used to be the same way with his wife. No matter what, he would not change his mind—whether it was where to go on a family trip or what to have for dinner. He was a keen sportsman when he was younger and was physically quite large—very much an alpha male character. He was raised to believe that changing his mind over a disagreement he had with his wife would mean "giving in" and result in some part of him being diminished. In fact, he didn't change his mind in disagreements with most people. Every time I would see him with his wife, they would bicker over what looked like trivial issues.

He finally realised—as I did—that it's futile to resist changing one's mind when it makes good sense to do so. For example, if he gets new information, has an insight or just re-examines a decision he has previously made, and this new data calls for a change of mind, it would be ridiculous not to change it. The feeling of resistance, of being stubborn, is once again clearly just a reflection of your thoughts in the moment. He also realised that his feelings of stubbornness and resistance were stopping him from seeing the situation as objectively as he might have done. Once my client experienced this, he became a changed man with a far smoother experience of life in his marriage, and he's done it without becoming a doormat.

Nowadays, I change my mind quite often. The need to do so normally occurs when I lose sight of the information I'm sharing in this book and I fall into one of my old misunderstandings. Often within a short amount of time I realise what has happened and I naturally take a different stance. You could say, I don't actually change my mind, but *I stop clinging to one particular point of view*. This has led me to see that our minds can change in an instant because our thinking changes from moment to moment. We can *stop* this natural process when we stubbornly hold on to a particular thought or belief, but we only do this because of our own misunderstandings.

Now there may be times when it makes sense to "stay the course." For example, if someone is pressuring you to change your point of view or stance but deep down you know that isn't the right thing to do, it's appropriate to have the courage of your convictions. Changing your mind isn't about giving up who you are. Again, the only problem is one of misunderstanding. Real strength doesn't come from whether or not you change your mind in the face of outside circumstances. Real strength is when you are willing to change your mind, which is far easier when we understand how our feelings reflect our thinking in the moment. Once you understand that and drop your misunderstandings, you allow your mind to function as it should. That way, if you know deep down that your decision is the right one, you will stick to it. If you know that it isn't, you can change your mind without making it a big deal.

This is as true in business as it is in personal relationships.

Some may say that this all boils down to ego. We will explore this idea in the next chapter.

CHAPTER 37.

Ego Is Made of Thought

Ego. A small word, and yet one that has been a huge part of my own misunderstandings for many years.

The philosopher and spiritual teacher Sydney Banks said, "Ego is only what you think you are and what you think of life, nothing more, nothing less."

This strikes me as such an accurate statement. Our ego is whatever we think about ourselves and of life. "Think" being the key word. It is not, however, who we actually are. In an earlier chapter I mentioned having an inkling of this when I was younger, and I believe deep down we all know that we are greater than our thinking.

One of my big misunderstandings—and I see this in my clients as well—is that we believe our thinking about ourselves. However, when we see that our thinking changes over time and that we have different thoughts every moment of every day, we can begin to understand that it doesn't determine who we actually are. But when we don't realise this, and instead allow our thoughts to convince us we are something else, we cause unnecessary problems for ourselves.

For example, I used to place a lot of value on my job, my salary and the benefits and title that came along with them. I thought my job was a key part of who I was—and I thought it meant I was "somebody." I thought it meant I had some importance because I earned more money than others, I had a nicer car than some people and I had some power in my job. This line of thought naturally came along with a fear that should this be taken away from me, I would be diminished. And this in turn stopped me from really shining and doing well because I didn't want to risk losing what my image was based on.

In my experience, dropping my misunderstandings seems to chip away at my ego. Rather than this hurting me, however, I have discovered that as my ego slowly diminishes it is replaced by something far greater, namely a deeper realisation of who I am beyond my ego: my true self. The irony is that we are all capable of greatness and our ego is what holds us back by fooling us into believing we are something we are not.

I never realised that I could do something about this. I thought my ego was a fixed entity. Sometimes I even thought it was a good thing that propelled me to excel. I understood in a "spiritual" way why some might argue that it wasn't good to have a big ego. But I didn't realise it held me back in a very real, practical sense.

I remember a senior manager at work once warning that the ego can get in the way of striking a good deal. But he also went on to say that while he had a large ego, this was okay because he knew about it. I took this to mean that ego can get in the way of success but it can also help you to be driven and to achieve. If this was true, then dropping the ego was of spiritual significance only, and doing so would not help me have greater success in work and life in general.

Looking back now I see that dropping of the ego—that is, dropping my misunderstandings—can only have a positive impact on success in every area of my life. If I drop ego in a business negotiation, I can create a better deal for my company than if I am blinded by my own ego. If one aspect of a negotiation makes me "look good" in the eyes of others and pleases my ego, I'm more likely to place a greater emphasis on that than I will on another aspect of the deal that's good for my company but which doesn't carry the same weight in the eyes of others.

I could write an entire book about ego, but for now I will simply point out that understanding how our minds really work is an antidote to our excessive egos. It results in seeing more clearly who you are and what you are capable of, and it leads to a much deeper experience of life.

Any thought you have right now that this is not true, or that it wouldn't work for you, is simply your own ego, your own misunderstanding, keeping you stuck. You are not your job, your age, your looks, your personality, your experience, your wealth or anything outside of you. You are far more than that. As you read these words, I know that a part of you knows this too.

Embrace it!

CHAPTER 38.

Dealing with Criticism

I tried for much of my life to please others, and one result of this was that I never wanted to be criticised. I would always play it safe. If I could avoid sticking my neck out, I could avoid being criticised and feeling bad about it.

Once I saw that criticism has nothing to do with my feelings, it made it much easier to simply play full-out.

These days I am quite visible within certain coaching circles. With being visible often comes criticism. For example, I am sure there are some who will not like this book. If this turns out to be the case, I can handle it in a couple of ways. In the past I would likely have gotten defensive or tried to justify why I'd written it the way I had. I would engage my intellect to try and fight against any criticism I received. Or, if that criticism "got to me" then I would feel sorry for myself and over-analyse the situation.

My attitude these days is a bit more nuanced. What I have come to see now is that criticism always presents the opportunity to learn and grow. Criticism shouldn't be something I need to avoid because it doesn't feel good. That doesn't make sense if we are only feeling our thinking moment to moment. For me, it now makes sense to listen to any criticism I receive, no matter what I feel in the moment I receive it, and then to look to see if there is anything I can learn from it. This may not happen immediately— as I am being criticised—but when I let my feelings in the moment of criticism pass, I often see something of value that can help me.

I recall a time when a former client criticised me. I felt awful about it. I pride myself on delivering an excellent service to my clients, and she was the first person to ever come back and tell me she was not satisfied. I felt at the time that I had done my best and she was being a little harsh, but when my mind eventually settled down—helped by what I know about how our feelings are reflections of our thoughts in the moment—I saw a couple of things I could do in the future to ensure that it would be less likely that a client would not be satisfied. I now look back at this situation as a wonderful gift. It reminds me of the Bill Gates quote: "Your most unhappy customers are your greatest source of learning."

I would add that they are your greatest source of learning, as long as you are willing to listen to them without taking it personally as an attack.

It's important to understand that this doesn't mean changing myself to please others. If, in an effort to stop being criticised, I tried to take on board all the criticism I ever received and change what I put out into the world, I would never please anybody.

On the other hand, if I say, "Well, criticism is the other person not understanding how their mind works," and so simply ignore it, I also miss out on the possibility for growth and development. Not getting caught up in the misunderstanding of how the mind works allows me (and you) to listen to what is useful, hear what can help us—and ignore what doesn't.

This is equally true whether the criticism comes from parents, society or our spouse. We can listen and decide that there is nothing to change, but we can also ask ourselves in such cases: are we *really* listening? I know when I was being criticised by my parents, I would simply hear, "You are not good enough"—and then stop listening. When I finally, truly paid attention to them, I heard: "We love you, we want the best for you, we are worried about you." I could then communicate with them differently, and also consider some points that they were right about.

This is often easier said than done, but it's worth it. When we change our relationship with criticism we remove a huge barrier to growth.

I spoke with a fellow coach recently who was putting on an event around better relationships. He had a great idea and was full of enthusiasm, but he wasn't making much progress in bringing it to reality. What I uncovered was that he wanted it all to be perfect—a side effect of not wanting criticism—and so wasn't moving forward. When I pointed out that this was holding him back, his misunderstanding cleared up and things started moving again. I see many coaches doing this with projects—from events to websites and more—where it's clear that if they were willing to move ahead with their projects when they felt they were 80 percent right they would have far greater success.

Misunderstanding around how your mind works makes you resist criticism and holds you back from the natural process of learning. Think about it: If we were born to avoid criticism, we would never have learned so many things as babies, toddlers and young children. How many times do you fall before you learn to walk? How many times do you mispronounce words before you learn to speak? When I shared my sweets as a child, I didn't stop myself for fear of being criticised.

Is there somewhere in your life where you're avoiding doing something out of fear of being criticised? How is your thinking in that area shaping what you're willing to do—or not do—to avoid criticism?

CHAPTER 39.

Your Own Capacity/Potential

I have been hinting throughout this book, that we all possess huge potential beyond what our minds may comprehend right now. I believe you are capable of far more than you realise in this moment.

You may ask me how I know this.

It's simple: I know because I've seen it time and again, both with clients and other people I've met. The only thing that gets in our way is that same misunderstanding about how our minds work.

I am not saying that we should all think positively. I am not making a blanket statement that makes a good quote for Facebook. I am instead pointing to a deeper truth that I see in all human beings.

You may think that some people think too much of themselves and overestimate their abilities. You may also think that people aren't all born with equal skillsets or innate abilities and that some people have genetic advantages. You are correct in all of that; however I don't believe this negates what I am pointing to.

Regardless of your race, your nationality, your existing talents and abilities, your gender or your age, I *know* that when you drop misunderstandings about the mind, about life and about who you are, huge potential opens up for you. What this looks like, I cannot tell you. It is different for each and every person, but I know that this is what happens. When we have misunderstandings about the mind, it is like driving a car with the handbrake on. Seeing those misunderstandings for what they are—and releasing the handbrake—can only make living (and driving) easier.

Another one of my clients offers a good case study of this process in action. Karen (not her real name) was studying at university and really struggling when we started coaching together. As we worked through many of the topics in this book, Karen started to get an understanding of how her mind works. One result was that her grades began to improve because she was less stressed about her studies. Then, when she graduated, she struggled to find a job. When we spoke she realised once again that her struggle was of her own creation; some of her misunderstandings about her own capabilities and self-worth fell away and she got herself a good job. After a while, she started to feel out of her depth, thinking maybe she wasn't cut out for her position. Once again, we spoke and found further misunderstandings about her ability to take on new challenges. Within weeks she had been promoted.

(Karen's case shows us that this process of letting go of misunderstandings doesn't always happen all at once, but it's reassuring that we can continue to grow and "remember" ourselves whenever we encounter challenges in life.)

I am a firm believer that even though there has been research on peak performance and personal growth for decades, we are really only scratching the surface of the process of tapping into our innate capacity to create in this world.

I occasionally ask my clients to stop and think about the following: given their experiences and their abilities, and without changing a thing, do they believe they are meeting their full potential?

Everyone I have asked tells me "no."

We all know, deep down, that we are capable of so much

more, but this knowledge is clouded over with misunderstandings about what's possible, who we are, and how we think the world works. It is often easier to see potential in others because our view of them is sometimes not quite so clouded by misunderstandings. Think about your best friend, or your colleague or someone else you know. Ask yourself, could they be experiencing greater success, happiness or just more of what they wanted if they dropped some of the thoughts about life that they were carrying around?

If the answer to that is yes, is it possible that the same could be true for you?

CHAPTER 40.

You Can Have What You Want

When I talk to people about the misunderstandings that I've shared in this book, they often wonder: if we accept the idea that we are simply experiencing our feelings through our thinking, doesn't this mean that we will lose our desire to create, achieve and accomplish certain goals? There is an underlying assumption that what motivates us to achieve a goal is the positive feeling we get when we achieve it. If this were not the case—if there wasn't going to be a positive feeling after we achieve a goal—surely we wouldn't try?

This may look like the case, and in fact some people do end up dropping certain goals they'd been chasing once some of their misunderstandings fall away. But this is because they had thought that achieving those goals would make them happy. Once they realise that happiness is not really connected to the achievement of their goals, they may change their behaviour, focus or direction. In other words, they may stop pursuing goals that they now realise are based on misunderstandings of what achievement of those goals would mean. However, what I have seen time and time again is that people who really see what we've been talking about in this book become more productive, more creative and often more energised than they were before.

When you look more closely, this makes a lot of sense. If we are staking our happiness on the achievement of a certain goal, we lose perspective. We put additional mental pressure on ourselves because our wellbeing relies on it. In this way, we make it much harder for ourselves to achieve whatever it is that we set out to achieve. I used to call this the "wanting-it tax". The more badly I wanted something, the more it seemed to elude me.

But the opposite holds true as well. The more relaxed we can be about achieving a certain goal, the easier it is for us to be creative, have fun and ultimately achieve what we want. If we don't achieve what we set out to, we can take on board any lessons learned and move forward without beating ourselves up. It makes sense that if the achievement of a goal doesn't have any impact on our wellbeing, on our happiness or self-worth, then it's far easier to approach our goals in a light-hearted way. And as we saw in the previous chapter, another side effect of our misunderstandings falling away is that we realise our own inner strength even more.

What occurs as a result of all this is that we end up with a lot more of what we really want in our lives.

I had a client who was desperately trying to find "the one" for him. Brian (not his real name) had tried all sorts of courses, read every book on the subject and spent a lot of money on trying to get this area of his life "handled." However, the harder he tried to find someone to spend his life with, the more this mystery person eluded him. He didn't know what to do and was on the verge of giving up. When I first introduced Brian to the possibility that meeting someone would have no impact on his happiness, he found it hard to believe. However, as we explored this idea and he started to see the truth of what I was pointing out to him, he started to relax. He stopped beating himself up and started enjoying life a lot more.

One day, out of the blue, he told me he had met the most amazing woman and they were now dating. He was surprised that when he took his attention away from meeting someone, he *did* meet someone. But this made complete sense to me. Why? Brian's desperation to meet his soul mate made it seem like he was wearing some kind of toxic aftershave. You can imagine him tripping all over himself when he met someone new, wondering if she was "the one" and if he would finally get what he so desperately wanted. But in his new relaxed outlook that kind of thinking didn't make sense and so didn't come up, and it made him much more attractive in the eyes of the woman he met.

You can perhaps see how Brian's process could apply in many other situations, such as wanting a new job or a promotion. Is there anything you are desperate to achieve that you may actually be keeping yourself away from through a similar kind of misunderstanding?

CHAPTER 41.

Racism Is No Exception

We all have certain subjects on which we seem less able to see clearly. For me, one such topic was racism. Whenever I encountered someone who was being racist or treating me differently because of the colour of my skin, I would get incredibly angry and upset. These feelings felt involuntary and I felt justified in feeling them. They seemed to indicate how wrong the "racist" was and how right I was.

For example, once, when I was a lot younger, a boy in my younger brother's class called him a derogatory, racist term (a "paki"). I got upset and started pushing him and asking him why he had called my brother that and would he dare say it to me. Even though I was only a few years older, I was a lot bigger than this boy. My actions got me into trouble. This boy's stepfather started pushing me and telling me to pick on someone my own size, but I wouldn't apologise or back down. I shouted at the father that his stepson had called my brother a "paki" and he didn't care. I felt even more angry. I felt like I was right. I needed to stand up to racists like this boy and his stepfather. I wished at the time that I was bigger so I could have punched the stepfather and told him that there is never an excuse for that kind of language. It seemed clear to me that my feelings were telling me how wrong the situation was and how much of a victim I was.

In similar situations, my father—although of course not a fan of racist behaviour—would be cool, calm and collected. He would tell me to ignore racist behaviour whenever I encountered it, to get my head down and simply get on with life. He told me that those who were acting racist were simply insecure—and demonstrating it through their actions. He had encountered racist behaviour—some that was shocking to me—as a young Indian boy growing up in England in the 60s and 70s, but he seemed to have moved on.

Now I could be level-headed and think clearly in many situations, but not when encountering this kind of behaviour. However, when I started to drop my misunderstandings around thinking, I slowly started to realise that this applied to racism too. There are no exceptions to my feeling my thinking from moment to moment. Therefore, my anger and upset at racist behaviour was not coming from the behaviour; it was coming from my own thinking about the behaviour. That makes sense and explains why, when encountering the same behaviour, my father could stay cool and calm while I would lose it.

Looking back at the situation with my younger brother, I see it could have been a great opportunity for dialogue with this young boy. To ask him why he called my brother a "paki", and what he thought that word meant. It could have been an opportunity to speak to this boy's parents, in a calm manner, and ask them whether it was common for them to use this language at home. We could have genuinely explored any misunderstandings they might have had around people of a different skin colour. Who knows, it could have led to them coming around for dinner and seeing that we are not so different after all. I see the wisdom of my father's advice now.

Given this, am I saying we shouldn't do anything about racists or their behaviour?

Actually, I'm not advocating what you should or shouldn't do. I'm simply saying that if we believe our upset feelings have anything to do with racism (or any other behaviour that appears to trigger us) then we are living in a misunderstanding and therefore acting less effectively than we might do without it. If we look at

South Africa after apartheid, for example, we see that the country healed not through anger, retaliation and retribution (for the most part) but through dialogue and genuine curiosity.

I also know that throughout all my years of anger, upset and feelings of historical injustices, I don't believe I changed anyone's views on race. Beyond this, it sure wasn't fun for me being upset. Since dropping those feelings I feel like I am a better role model to support changing the views others may have of me based on the colour of my skin or where my parents were born. Whether anyone changes their views or not, it does not have an impact on my life or how I feel. I have a far better experience of life when I don't get caught out by this particular flavour of misunderstanding.

Do you have areas in life or certain topics where you see red, which could be based on simple misunderstandings?

CHAPTER 42.

Planning (Is It Necessary?)

Given the misunderstandings I've been pointing to in this book, you might think you just need to wait for a "nice feeling" to take action. Many people do. Maybe you think that when you're feeling anxious, upset, nervous or insecure, these are signs that you aren't seeing clearly—so you should wait until you *are* seeing clearly before you take whatever action you're feeling nervous about.

This is, again, another misunderstanding.

If you're organising a party, it makes sense to plan ahead and organise things that are best taken care of in advance. Similarly, when you are undertaking a project, especially a complex one, it often makes sense to plan ahead and anticipate the actions you need to take at various times to achieve the outcome you want. You could do this for a complex business project or when organising a family holiday. I have personally spent more time planning projects now than I did before I was introduced to the nature of my thinking.

There is however, a benefit to dropping any misunderstandings about your thinking or feelings around the realm of planning. Many, if not most, projects don't go exactly to plan. When this happens it can seem that this causes you to feel anxious, stressed or uncomfortable. If this looks like reality to you, you may end up rigidly sticking to a plan that is outdated, or you might make snap decisions out of insecurity and stress.

Obviously, this may not be the best way to proceed.

However, understanding that we can only be feeling our thinking moment to moment—and not the effects of the given situation in which we find ourselves—can lead us towards clarity in moments where those around us are panicking, stressed and upset.

I've already mentioned my client Ian, an IT project manager. Ian lived in the world of complex plans, but in a way his schedule seemed to control him more than he controlled his schedule. He managed teams and was constantly stressed, overworked and tired. It seemed to him that in his world there was no other option except to be stressed and work incredibly long hours. He then managed his stress through various addictions: smoking, food and computer games. He used to guzzle down large quantities of energy drinks every day.

When he first reached out to me, he wanted things to change but he couldn't understand how to bring it about. I shared some resources with him which reinforced what I was telling him about how the mind really works. He slowly started to see how his misunderstandings—as opposed to his workload, deadlines, and colleagues—were causing him to feel stressed. This is when things began to change.

Projects started to run smoother, his communication with senior colleagues and stakeholders improved, and he was even able to take some time off for a holiday. Better planning started to take place naturally as his mind became clearer. Not only was his wife happier with the change, but he was far less stressed at work and he started to enjoy his job again. In his personal life, his planning skills had been equally poor, but as he saw through his misunderstandings in his professional life, he started to plan better in his personal life too. Flights were no longer booked two days before he was due to fly, bills were paid on time and he showed up to social engagements at the right time as well. This was something he had believed was simply not possible.

Not only this but I noticed that in my Immersions he was

drinking water rather than sugary drinks, and in the evenings he usually chose to get an early night rather than join others for a beer. This change did not happen overnight, but once he saw something that was true, it was hard for him to *unsee* it. The poor planning had been a symptom rather than the real issue, and when we started to address his relationship to his thinking, there were many knock-on effects.

Have you ever avoided planning a holiday, a project or even your workday or work week because your mind was already racing? As we begin understanding how our minds really work, our misunderstandings fall away and we see what we need to do more clearly—so we naturally do it. Planning becomes natural to us because it is based on a new understanding of what we need to do to achieve our goals, rather than as a way to manage stress in our lives.

CHAPTER 43.

The Media Innocently Promotes Misunderstanding

As I've shared throughout this book, many people believe events and circumstances have the power to make them feel something. You only have to watch the news or read the newspaper to see this. Almost every article or news story points to our feelings being created by something other than our own thinking.

You can do this exercise yourself. Pick up any newspaper and see if there are articles that imply that your feelings are being caused by something outside of you. "Property investors fear higher interest rates", "Stock market slump panics investors", "President furious about troop movements", "Fans devastated as team loses trophy in final game of the season" and so on. From the front page to the sports section at the back, articles and headlines seem to agree that our feelings are coming from outside of us or that certain circumstances can evoke particular feelings. As the headlines above indicate, this could be in the form of worry about the economy, fear over terrorists, or joy at the local sports team winning a trophy.

I believe this is innocent and I am not blaming the media. We have all been brought up with this misunderstanding. I felt the same way until I realised that the world doesn't work this way. We are not at the mercy of outside events in the way these headlines imply. But when so much of our culture is based on the misunderstanding that the outside world directly impacts our experience of life, it's no wonder this is so easy to miss and why people may feel fearful of what they read in the papers or watch on the news. This is despite the world tending to get better across a whole range of indicators. (Just do a quick internet search of Hans Rosling, who was a Swedish physician, academic, statistician, and public speaker, and check out some of his videos using good-quality data to show how the world is becoming healthier, safer and more wealthy).

The same is true, by the way, with any pop song you can find. Artists singing about heartbreak caused by a romantic partner, or the joy of finding the "one" or leaving the "wrong one"—none of this makes sense when we really start to see how our minds work, and yet it is so compelling. The American rapper Skee-Lo wrote a song called "I Wish," which starts with the lyrics

I wish I was a little bit taller
I wish I was a baller
I wish I had a girl who looked good, I would call her

The whole song is about things he wishes were different in his life, with the underlying message being if they were he would be happier and life would be better.

I forget this regularly myself, to the point where I can feel, for example, that someone winning a particular political office causes me to feel upset or worried. The media can encourage this through headlines like "Disappointment for many with narrow loss for candidate X in the polls" or "Shock as politician defies the polls to win by the narrowest of margins". However, life and my feelings don't work this way; when I recover my understanding of this, I drop the fears and anxiety.

I often feel that the world is becoming more and more polarised, with people identifying as left wing or right wing, conservative or liberal. When we don't understand what our feelings are telling us, we can become really entrenched in our points of view; we'll only engage with the media that supports our existing beliefs and refrain from open dialogue with people holding different opinions. We believe that our feeling of certainty about an issue means we are right and the other person is wrong, stupid or morally corrupt.

Yet once I see that my feelings aren't telling me that I am right and someone else is wrong—they are only reflecting my thinking in the moment—I can tap back into my curiosity and better understand other people's points of view.

I recently spoke with a man who lived in the US and who was very pro-gun. The UK media generally portrays pro-gun Americans as short-sighted and caring more about gun rights than they do about the lives of children. I didn't understand how anyone could be so avidly pro-gun. Yet knowing that whatever he told me couldn't make me feel anything, and knowing that I didn't need to change his mind to feel better, I started to ask him questions about his views. What did he feel the media left out of their presentation? What were his views on greater legislation and background checks? We had a great conversation marked by mutual respect. I learned more about why he thought what he did, and he even opened up to some ideas different from those typically associated with people of his political persuasion. This was a great reminder for me that everyone has different thoughts; I can only get a glimpse of what is going on in their heads, but it's a lot more clear when I drop my misunderstandings.

I remember once getting my hair cut in London. I was sitting in a small barber's shop near Waterloo train station. It looked like it hadn't changed at all in over twenty years. The barber who cut my hair was really worried because of what he had been hearing in the news about terrorists. It seemed clear to him that London was becoming a much more dangerous city to live in. I, on the other hand, lived very close to his barber shop and felt it was the safest neighbourhood in which I had ever lived. I found people to be incredibly friendly. Neither of us had ever personally encountered any terrorism. So it wasn't terrorism causing my barber to feel afraid, but his thoughts about terrorism. By the same token, my own thoughts were causing me to feel safe.

I mentioned the work of Hans Rosling above. In the same vein, if you feel I might be misguided about terrorism, check out the website ourworldindata.org. Here, Max Roser, an economist at the Institute for New Economic Thinking at Oxford University, presents real-world data showing that long-term trends indicate things have gotten better in terms of global health, access to food and decreased violence. Even as the media covers violent wars around the globe, war deaths are declining at a rapid pace. And working hours per week have declined significantly over the past one hundred years.

You may wonder: are these statistics really accurate? Do we truly live in a safer world? The fact is that our *feelings* are *not* an indication of the answer to these questions. Our misunderstandings are what cause so many people to live from a place of fear as opposed to using our natural intelligence to respond appropriately to our world.

Look back at your own life and think about things that you were really concerned and worried about that you might have heard or read in the media a few years ago. Did they turn out as badly as you thought they would?

This is not to say we should remain unresponsive to the challenges that exist in the world today. But understanding our thinking and emotional responses to our daily doses of media allows us a great deal more perspective on issues, and this generally leads to more effective action.

CHAPTER 44.

Don't Give Your Power Away

If you believe the world works "outside-in" and that your feelings are telling you about your circumstances or anything else happening "out in the world", then you are far easier to control and manipulate. You are, in fact, giving your power away and losing connection with your own common sense.

Imagine for a moment that other people or circumstances DO have the power to make you feel a certain way. Let's explore a couple of examples.

If carrots caused you to feel rage, all someone would need to do to make you lose your temper is place some carrots in front of you. You would be infuriated, and there would be nothing you could do about it. The only logical course of action would be to get as far away from them as possible in order to calm down again. If cucumbers made you afraid, all anyone need do to control you would be to show you one and have you cower in fear. They could trap you in your house by planting cucumbers all around your garden. They could get you to do what they wanted by threatening you with cucumbers!

Yes, these examples are silly, but it doesn't take a big leap to see that this is the way things often play out in real life. People often lose their temper at things that have no power to make them feel angry or are afraid of things that can't cause them harm. I recently met a man who told me he used to get into fights simply because someone looked at him. He used to operate as if that look had the power to make him angry, so he would go and fight that person. If we examine this scenario closely, it makes about as much sense as getting angry when you see a carrot.

Again, I am not saying we should just stick our heads in the sand and not pay attention to the world. But when we fall prey to the misunderstanding that people and circumstances have the power to make us feel a certain way, we are giving away our power to engage meaningfully with the world around us.

We are born powerful. I spoke about this during an interview for a recent podcast, saying:

"The problem isn't that you're not powerful. It isn't that you don't know how to do what it is that you want to do. You are *far, far more powerful* than you realise. The only problem you've got is that you've believed a bunch of thoughts about yourself which simply aren't true."

Take a moment to reflect on these words. What would happen if you simply stopped believing all the thoughts you had about you not being good enough, not being clever enough, wealthy enough, strong enough, attractive enough or loveable enough?

CHAPTER 45.

What Happens when You're Offended?

A few years ago I watched comedian Steve Hughes talk about being offended. He made a great point: if you're offended, nothing happens. You're just offended.

Apart from finding this funny, I realised he was making a very valid point. Many of us get upset when we feel offended by something someone else has said or done. But being offended is entirely subjective. We aren't all offended by the same things, and what offends us today may not even offend us a few years from now—and vice versa. Maybe when we were younger we told a silly joke that we wouldn't find funny today. My favourite joke when I was younger was about a magic slide. Whatever you said while you went down the slide, you landed in it. The joke went that some people said gold, diamonds or money—and then a little boy slid down the slide yelling "wee!" I found that joke so funny for years until one day I no longer did and considered it childish. (Now I admit I find it funny again!)

Perhaps once upon a time if someone was short with us we'd immediately take offense and think they had no manners, but nowadays if the same thing happens we might assume they are having a bad day—and we don't take it personally. When I was a teenager, I often made up stories about others being rude to me. Someone might ask if they could help me when I entered a shop and I would make up a story that they thought I was a shoplifter. Now I enjoy it when I enter a shop and someone asks if they can help me. In each of these cases, it's our thoughts that determine whether we're offended or not.

When we view being offended through the lens of the misunderstandings around thought, it's clear that the feeling of being offended is just a feeling. It's an indicator of our thinking. Nothing more. And like all other feelings, it's not telling us how offensive something is. All it's telling us is that we feel offended based on our thinking in that moment.

Knowing this gives us a huge amount of perspective and personal power.

If for example, I am offended by a certain political candidate's comments and I don't realise that I am actually feeling offended because of my *thinking* about their comments, when I hear their rhetoric I have no choice but to feel offended. I blame my feeling of being offended on what I hear. But if I know that this feeling of being offended is *just* a feeling then I don't need to do anything about it. I may realise the candidate has different views from me. I may think they are misguided. But I don't need to waste my energy being offended by them.

In fact, being offended often has an interesting way of playing out in the world. Many times fringe political parties are given more airtime and coverage because numerous people are offended by them. If no-one paid them any attention, they would be more likely to simply fall by the political wayside. You can think of your own "offended" feelings the same way—stop giving them coverage and they'll fall by the wayside.

Allow me to reiterate something I've said several times already. I am not saying you shouldn't stand up for yourself or to people who are spouting hate. My goal is not to direct you to engage in any particular type of action. What I *am* saying is that if you take action based on the idea that someone else is responsible for offending you, then you are misguided. Any actions you take based on those feelings may actually turn out to be counterproductive. I discussed my own experience of this in the chapter on racism.

Imagine someone or something that has offended you in the past. How would you react differently if you hadn't felt offended by what was said or done, or if the feeling of being offended was fleeting and only lasted momentarily?

CHAPTER 46.

Generosity Is Innate

I didn't consider myself a particularly generous person growing up. I didn't see the point, and I thought I'd be taken advantage of. However, I also didn't want others to think I *wasn't* generous—because I cared so much what they thought of me. I tried to walk a fine line, pretending not to care what others thought (while caring) and always hoping to get a good deal.

I especially remember not being happy about splitting the bill on a night out if my food and drinks costs less than the average. I would not speak up, though, and suggest we pay for what we ordered, because I was so concerned about what others would think. I would imagine people thinking I was "tight-fisted" or miserly quibbling over a few pounds.

In my twenties I found that many of the people I admired were extremely generous. This seemed like a revelation to me, so I thought I had to cultivate generosity within myself to be liked and appreciated, just as these other people were. This took some effort on my part, but in the end nothing much really changed. Perhaps I just wasn't the generous type? Maybe it wasn't in my personality?

I had of course forgotten the generosity I displayed as a very young boy when I shared my sweets with my new friend.

I gradually realised that the reason I found it difficult to be more generous was because I saw it as giving away a resource—money—that was finite. I believed that money had the power to make me feel good. Conversely, lack of money seemed to have the ability to make me feel bad. Since I wanted to feel good, I found it difficult to be generous.

I found the same was true of being generous with my time, which I also felt was a finite resource. If I chose to use it effectively, it could make me feel better, so giving it away to others seemed illogical. Why would I trade my happiness for someone else's?

As I started to see that my feelings were just a reflection of my thinking in the moment—and that time, money and everything else had no power to make me feel anything at all—I naturally grew more generous. I realised it was within my nature to help others, to share what I had—just as I had done when I was a young boy. The only thing that had been getting in my way was my misunderstanding about what money and time meant.

I came to see that these ideas applied to other things as well—food, for example. I was brought up in a bustling household. When food was on the table, we ate. First come, first served. I "learned" that certain foods had the ability to make me feel good, so it was important to eat them. I didn't see that food could be shared without detriment to my happiness. There is a great scene in the hit 90s TV show *Friends* where the character Joey stops dating a girl because she picks at the food on his plate. He shouts at her "Joey doesn't share food!" I could relate to that myself until I saw that there was no connection between food and happiness. Now it's easy to share my food, and to be generous in other ways as well.

This shift around generosity also happened for a client of mine. Alyssa was quite wealthy and always very careful with her money. Despite having the financial means to be generous, she never seemed to be—until she, too, started to see through her misunderstandings around money. Alyssa had always thought that because she had made money as a businesswoman, she didn't have misunderstandings around money. She thought she understood the ins and outs of the financial arena. (She was a shrewd and effective businesswoman.) However, as we worked together she came to realise that she had placed a lot of value on her having money; she thought that it gave her a sense of importance. When Alyssa realised that money itself was neutral, these thoughts of her self-worth as related to money fell away, and she started to be more generous and giving with those around her. She found that she enjoyed helping others.

I remember never giving money to homeless people because I was told that they would just spend it on alcohol or drugs. There was also a part of me that felt I didn't have enough so I didn't want to give away what I had. I also heard a story when I was a teenager of a man who begged in London but had a professional job during the day. He apparently made thousands of pounds as a professional beggar while not needing the money. These stories gave me an excuse to not be generous to people I saw on the streets.

Then a few years ago, I was walking in Birmingham city centre during winter. It was bitterly cold and I saw a man who must have been freezing. My heart went out to him, and without all the stories in my head about money or scams, I bought him some hot food and drink from a fast food restaurant nearby. The thought crossed my mind: what if this guy were my brother? Would I walk on by?

So many stories and thoughts we have about others get in the way of our natural generosity. Our thoughts of fairness, of whether someone deserves something or whether they will reciprocate. Not holding on to these thoughts so tightly—which is easier once I know they will pass anyway—means I am naturally more generous more of the time.

What if you truly saw money as neutral and as having no ability to make you feel anything? What if you dropped all of your thinking about what being more generous would mean? Would you be more generous or less?

CHAPTER 47.

Can Money Make You Unhappy?

I have touched on the idea of money throughout this book. This is because it's a subject that really seems to catch people out, both in terms of thinking money can make you happy and also that it can make you miserable. (It caught me out numerous times and in different guises).

One of my early clients was a young lady named Bethany. Bethany was looking to get a better job. However, it was clear to me that she had some deep (and I think fairly common) misunderstandings around money. Bethany would often mention people who earned what she thought was a lot of money but who were also unhappy. In her mind, therefore, she had determined that if she were to earn more money, she would be sacrificing some of her own happiness as a trade-off. I could relate to that misunderstanding from my days working in an office job! I thought if I got promoted, I'd have to work longer hours and as a result be less happy. The irony was, I often found myself bored in the evenings and spent time binge-watching TV shows online or playing games on my mobile phone.

I said to Bethany, "So you've said you know some wealthy people who are unhappy. Do you know poor people who are happy?"

She nodded. "Yes."

"How about this: do you know any wealthy people who *are*

happy, or poor people who aren't?"

With this question it began to dawn on her that she was only seeing part of the whole picture. If she knew people who were happy, sad and in between, irrespective of their wealth, then money was not really an indicator of happiness. She had been carrying around her own misunderstanding around money, and it was beginning to fall away.

After this, Bethany's path became much clearer. She studied to gain the qualifications she needed to move ahead in her career. Within twelve months she had a much higher-paying job than before and found that she really enjoyed it. Another twelve months later she told me that pointing out her misunderstandings around how too much money would cause her to feel unhappy or discontented was a turning point for her. Until then she was subconsciously sabotaging her earning potential because she wanted to stay happy.

Conversely, another one of my early clients, Jon, was a successful businessman who loved earning lots of money. In fact, he had done incredibly well for himself, had won awards for his business and was making more money than most of his peers. However, Jon was completely miserable and stressed. He felt stuck. The thought of earning less money was not an option, and working as hard as he did wasn't good for his health or sanity. Something needed to give.

While I did not coach Jon directly on the subject of money, I started to open him up to the role of his mind in his perceived problems. I asked him, why was he working so hard, and what the money meant for him. He told me that it was because he wanted to provide a good standard of life for his family. I gently suggested that he was hardly seeing his baby son or wife and had lost sight of what was important. Realising this led to changes in his behaviours at work, and he started going home on time and spending evenings with his family. Interestingly as his focus changed, his income did not drop. By taking the pressure off himself to earn as much as he did (or more), he became more creative and open-minded. This led to him learning how to delegate certain tasks to his staff, to streamline his own processes, and to become more efficient.

Where in your life do you confuse money with happiness or unhappiness, and what would happen if you dropped this misunderstanding?

CHAPTER 48.

Hard Work Doesn't Have to Be Hard

A similar misunderstanding exists around the concept of hard work. I held this particular one myself earlier in my own life and career. I felt that in order to earn more money, I needed to work harder. I saw the senior executives in my company leaving work after me and coming in earlier than me, even though they often had longer commutes. The underlying assumption was that working harder and longer would mean less enjoyment of life for me—but more money.

It was ironic that when I was home in the evenings I would often find myself bored. I was determined not to work too hard, and yet when I had free time I struggled to make the best use of that time.

I started to see two misunderstandings.

Firstly, it was not true that the only way to earn more money was to work harder. In fact, when I examined my own career up to that point, it was clear that I wasn't necessarily working harder every time my pay increased. Instead, my work tended to go through cycles that were often out of my control.

Secondly, even if I did work harder, or for longer hours, this was in no way related to my own level of happiness or satisfaction with life. I see this especially clearly now because I really enjoy the work I currently do. I don't mind working in the evenings, for example, writing this book.

What I didn't realise at the time was that these two

misunderstandings were holding me back from greater success in my career and earnings. I would subconsciously not apply for roles that would pay more because I thought it would mean working harder and being less happy. I saw this as a direct trade-off. It was a version of the misunderstanding that Bethany, my client from the last chapter, had about wealthier people being less happy.

Enjoyment from our jobs and careers doesn't come from the work that we do. Any task that you currently don't enjoy in your job would be something that someone else probably loves to do. Even the worst job you have ever held would be something that someone else would love to have. Once we stop attributing our feelings of satisfaction, joy and wellbeing to coming from the work we do, we are free to truly enjoy our work. Thinking that a particular job or career will make you happy is essentially the same misunderstanding as thinking the perfect partner would make you happy, or the right car or the right weather will make you feel satisfied.

Have you ever put off a certain task at work because you thought it was difficult, boring, mundane or something similar, only to find that once you started the task it wasn't that bad?

I once coached a young man called Steve who was struggling to get a job. He had trained for a particular career path but there were very few opportunities in that field once he graduated. He did, however, have the opportunity to take up a sales job. But because he thought he would be more satisfied working in the field in which he was trained, he sat unemployed. I coached him around this subject and explored the thinking that had him only wanting to work in the field he was trained in. This conversation opened his mind up to taking on the sales job, even if it was only for the short term. He started earning a good wage for the first time in his life and even got promoted twice within a few months. He started enjoying his job and saw it in a completely different light.

Am I suggesting that we should just take on any job because

no job has the power to make us feel anything?

No.

What I am suggesting is that we often have a lot of unconscious thinking around work and certain career paths which may limit what we do in our careers. Being aware of this can open us up to jobs and careers we may not have considered and which we may end up excelling in. On the flip side, I have seen many people searching for the ideal role or career that they think will make them feel fulfilled, only to keep searching endlessly or take on a role that doesn't do for them what they expect it to do.

CHAPTER 49.

You Don't Need to Be Appreciated

I used to believe that getting positive feedback from my boss was important to make me feel motivated and happy at work. I once took a personality test that confirmed this. In my mind, the need to be appreciated was simply a fact and not something that could be attributed to my thinking. This was a big area of misunderstanding for me not only in the work arena but also with my parents.

That said, at first it wasn't a problem at work because for many years I worked for bosses who gave me positive feedback when I had done well. I enjoyed this; it made me feel valued as an employee, and it motivated me to work harder. But when I began working for someone who wasn't as forthcoming in a positive way, my enthusiasm waned. This new boss seemed to spend more time telling me what I hadn't done well, and no matter how hard I tried to change it looked like things were out of my control. I felt increasingly demotivated.

So I instead tried to control my boss. I took it upon myself as my personal mission to show him how he needed to change to get the most/best out of me. I would directly tell him how his behaviours were demotivating me in our weekly catch-up meetings, I would share my personality profiles with him. I even asked for support from *his* boss, who sympathised with me. Part of me thought if he could change, I would be doing him a favour in helping him be a better manager and leader. My belief was that no one would be motivated working for someone like him who didn't spend enough time praising the good work of his employees.

As you can probably guess, this didn't work too well. I really felt like my next logical step was to resign or switch teams. Then I spoke to a mentor of mine (Dr. Keith Blevens) who asked me whether my boss not giving me the positive feedback I wanted was really causing me to feel unappreciated. I said, "Of course!"

Dr. Blevens pointed out my misunderstanding: this is not how we experience our reality. My feeling unappreciated was coming from inside me, a reflection of my thinking in the moment, and not as a result of my boss' behaviour.

This was a defining moment for me. This wasn't the first time this understanding—and my own misunderstandings—had been pointed out to me. But my boss and his being quite critical of me had been my blind spot. He was the exception to the rule. When Dr. Blevens helped me to see that even my feelings about my boss were nothing to do with him and were simply a reflection of my thinking in the moment, I saw just how pervasive my misunderstandings were. How easily we can be fooled by our thinking.

This was one of those times when I realised that *there are no exceptions*. At that moment, I truly saw that 100 percent of my experience is created by my thinking and it was that knowing that changed everything.

When my boss and I had a meeting and he spent 95 percent of the time telling me what I hadn't done well, I often felt irritation, anger and upset. It occurred to me that if these feelings weren't really telling me about my boss' behaviour, then were my thoughts of him being the worst boss I had worked for worth taking seriously?

I noticed that every time I was upset with my boss I had a *lot* of negative thoughts about him. So my first step was to give these negative thoughts less importance. I found as a result that my bad mood passed much more quickly, and I started to have new thoughts about how my boss was from a different culture and that he was managing me the best way he knew how. I no longer saw him as an ineffective boss but instead as a human being doing what made sense to him. I softened and stopped trying to change him. Eventually I stopped taking it personally when he was critical, and our relationship healed dramatically. I even started finding it amusing when he would, predictably, not praise me for a job well done.

This particular kind of misunderstanding was further highlighted for me a couple of years later when I was speaking to my best friend. He was struggling with an employee of his who wanted appreciation. He didn't understand why someone would want appreciation from their boss as he himself didn't feel the need to have it. He was more motivated by financial compensation as opposed to appreciation. Consequently he was trying to motivate his employee financially and couldn't understand why his approach wasn't working. I smiled as I saw the flip side of my misunderstanding and how my best friend was very similar to my old boss.

My old boss was managing me the way *he* would have liked to be managed by *his* boss. By taking my thinking about him so seriously I hadn't been able to appreciate that he thought differently from me and that his actions weren't personal.

This pattern was similar to one I had with my parents. I craved love and affection from them, especially from my father. I felt like I never received it, and when I brought it up with them, they didn't seem to understand what I was saying. My father would say, "You know that I love you; you don't need me to tell you."

It was only when I started to understand how I was creating my felt experience of life that I saw how much they did indeed love me and that they were doing the best they could, just as I was. My father wasn't withholding his love from me. In fact, looking back I saw so many times when he sacrificed so much for me and my siblings. However, as I was attributing my feelings of unhappiness and unworthiness to him, I was unable to see this. It is no surprise that my relationship with both my parents improved as I stopped trying to change them or judge them for not making me feel loved. If I am feeling my thinking then it no longer made sense to change them. By my not trying to change my parents, my arguments with them lessened and more positive, loving feelings for them arose inside of me.

I was once working with a client on the subject of romantic relationships. I asked him whether his ideal partner would be someone who loved him unconditionally, someone who didn't take offence when he was in a bad mood and said something he didn't mean. Someone who just loved him no matter what. He said, "Yes." I asked him if *he* was like that in his relationships or whether he was constantly evaluating the other person.

The penny dropped. We then went deeper as I asked him whether he was like that with himself. He realised just how critical he had been of his own behaviour and clearly saw that he wasn't as loving as he might have been to himself. I sometimes ask my clients, if you spoke to others the way you spoke to yourself, would you have better or worse relationships?

My client hadn't intended to make any of his former partners feel unappreciated, nor had they likely intended anything of the sort for him. Most people don't set out to make each other feel unappreciated. The feeling of appreciation or unappreciation comes from our own thinking. When we understand this we don't need to take it seriously if it seems that someone isn't as loving or appreciative of us as we would like. Paradoxically, if we *don't* overreact we are more likely to garner appreciation than we would be if we get upset when we don't receive it.

How would your professional and personal relationships change if you didn't need to be appreciated by anyone else, and if you could appreciate others regardless of how they treated you?

CHAPTER 50.

You Are Resilient by Design

In 2009 I read an article about resilience in an industry magazine. It was becoming more and more important—according to the article—for people to be resilient in the modern workplace, to recover from failure and rise to challenges. The article was even accompanied by a short questionnaire that determined what a reader's "resilience quotient" was, and it pointed to a book designed to help improve an individual's resilience through changing their behaviours.

When I started learning about how our minds work, I listened to interviews with people who already understood the material I've been discussing in this book. One of those interviews was with Cheryl Bond, a Doctor of Education who had worked with a very large defence contractor in the US. Cheryl was part of a team of people who designed a curriculum of leadership programs based on this new paradigm of psychology and taught in those programs for over a decade. One of the key benefits of these programs had been a significant increase in the resilience of the employees and the leaders. What fascinated me was that unlike the article I had read some years earlier, the training Cheryl and her colleagues delivered didn't focus on changing behaviours at all. Instead, Cheryl pointed out that we are all innately resilient. As human beings we have the ability to bounce back from setbacks that life seems to put in our way, and we may all have experienced some situation where—despite us thinking we couldn't cope—we *did* cope and ended up surprising ourselves.

I had never thought of resilience in this way. These same thoughts were mirrored for me when I later spoke with a woman named Cathy Casey, who has trained many people in this understanding from all walks of life, including prison inmates in California. Once again, Cathy saw that resilience is not something we attain through changing our behaviours; rather, it is already built into us.

Resilience is natural and we see it in children regularly, not least as they learn to talk, walk and play. They may "fail" by falling over, mispronounce words or make other mistakes, but they don't dwell on these failures and then give up. We also hear of remarkable stories of resilience in the news of people who are resilient in the face of extreme circumstances like war, famine or being stranded on a desert island.

I was recently speaking with a client whose business had suffered a major setback. He oscillated between thinking his life was a complete mess and feelings of bravado and overconfidence. I started to speak to him about how his mind really worked, how he was experiencing his thinking in the moment, and not his circumstances, and how his feelings of overconfidence and despair were both coming from the same place: his mind. Neither of these feelings was telling him about his business or his future earning potential.

His racing mind started to slow down and he began to get more clarity about his situation. In the space of one conversation, he started to feel more hopeful about things. This came down not to some misguided belief about his business but through seeing that he still had all the skills he had had before, that he had earning ability outside of his business, and that his costs were really manageable. It was all common sense, but before he had been lost in and paralysed by his overthinking. Now his natural resilience began coming through again.

When we see that our feelings are not created by our circumstances, we are naturally more resilient. Instead of giving up our power, you could say we are reclaiming it. On the flip side, if our feelings were determined, even in some small part, by our outside circumstances, then it would make it much harder to be resilient. We'd constantly be battling to stay positive despite being at the mercy of circumstances beyond our control. Instead, when we know that our feelings change constantly—because our thinking does—it makes sense that we can handle whatever life throws at us.

How resilient would you be if nothing could make you feel good or bad and if you knew that you would always be okay no matter what?

CHAPTER 51.

Why?

As a coach, I am trained to delve a little deeper when a client tells me what they want to achieve or create, or when they tell me about a problem they want to solve. A simple question that often provides profound insights—and one which young children also know to ask—is "Why?" Why do clients want to make more money? Why do they want to improve their relationships? Why do they want to find their true purpose or meet the man of their dreams?

We often don't stop to consider why we want certain things. It probably seems obvious to us.

"Well of course I don't need to explain why I want a Ferrari!"

It's always interesting for me to ask this question and hear my client's answer. More often than not, I hear a version of "Because this will make me feel better." Sometimes it can be a few layers deeper. For example, a client may think that if he buys a Ferrari he will be seen as a success in his father's eyes and that he will finally earn his respect. Subconsciously, he may feel that earning his father's respect will finally make him feel good enough—that is, better than he feels at present.

Now if it were true that achieving a goal would make us feel better, then it would make sense to go and achieve that goal. Absolute sense, in fact, because I believe all human beings just want to feel good. This even goes for people who partake in what looks like self-destructive behaviour, like using alcohol and drugs. On some level I believe they do so because they want to feel better.

The same reasoning applies to fixing any problems we might have; if doing so would stop us feeling bad, solving them makes sense.

However, if this is *not* how our psychology works, then that approach makes no sense at all. "But," you might say, "I *want* to feel good!" The thing is that feeling great is natural. We don't have to *strive* for it; it's simply what our mind reverts to when we aren't overthinking things. That's what we all did as children. We would revert back to our default state of happiness and contentment over and over again without us "doing" anything. Therefore I point out to clients that if their goal is ultimately to feel good, there is a much easier and more effective way to get there. Why?

Because there is nowhere to get to, and that feeling is just a thought away.

Feeling good does not occur from thinking happier thoughts—it comes about as a side effect of dropping our existing misunderstandings about our thinking. Another way of saying this is that it is a side effect of having a quieter mind, which is what we end up with when we see how our minds actually work.

I used to chase good feelings through all sorts of goals—a promotion, more money, a romantic partner, trying to have others treat me a certain way, power, respect, authority and, of course, a nice car! Whenever I achieved a certain goal, I would at best feel good for a short while. I didn't realise that I was caught up in a misunderstanding of where my good feelings come from. I also didn't realise that when I thought my good feelings were coming from something outside of me, I was often making it *more* difficult to achieve the goal I was trying to achieve.

Paradoxically, thinking for example that a promotion will make you happy often hampers you; you put a lot of pressure on yourself to get the promotion and this interferes with your ability to perform at your best. But when you drop this misunderstanding around happiness, you remove that interference and goals are more easily achieved. When I did this for myself I got a great job, started my own business, made money, met my dream girl and had much better relationships with everyone in my life. I have seen the same types of things happen with my clients.

We cannot get enough of what we don't need.

Not seeing this can often lead to people just wanting more and more of what they think will make them happy. A friend of mine bought a Porsche sports car as his reward for making so much money. He felt good for about two weeks until the feeling faded. A couple of years later, he went out and bought a more expensive sports car, a Ferrari. This was his ultimate dream car. However, the good feeling he was looking for didn't last either because no car can be the source of good feelings.

I invite you now to pause for a minute and think about a goal you're reaching for. Now ask yourself:

"Why?"

CHAPTER 52

Fasting and Giving Up Luxuries

For Roman Catholics around the world, Ash Wednesday marks the start of Lent. This is the forty-day period before Easter often associated with Christians fasting or giving things up—luxuries like chocolate or french fries. While I am not a Christian, and many of you reading this may not be either, I invite you to think about what you might like to give up, starting today, that could have the biggest positive impact on your life. Would it be sweets? Alcohol? Or something else altogether?

I recently asked a young man I was coaching, "Who would you be if you dropped all your stories and beliefs about yourself?" He wasn't really sure how to answer that question, but he knew there would be a shift in his life. He knew that his beliefs about himself were holding him back on some level. I believe that nearly everyone on the planet knows they have misunderstandings that hold them back too. What if, rather than giving up chocolate or carbs or fasting, we gave up our misunderstandings of who we really are and how the world works? Being open and willing to explore this question makes a huge difference to whether this book can help you.

I believe that deep down we all know we are not our bank balance, our job title, our car or even our body. It is the misunderstanding that we *are* these things that ultimately keeps us small, that stops us from shining brightly and fulfilling our potential.

One of my clients was a business owner who made a lot of money online but who had very poor relationships in his life. This was true with his romantic partner, his family and those who worked for him. He believed money and the luxuries he could buy with it would make him happy, would make him feel enough. He also felt that if people didn't behave the way he wanted them to, this would cause him to feel upset.

If you've read this far in this book, you know—or are, I hope, beginning to see—that neither of those things are true. Once my client started to see this truth as well, his business and general wellbeing improved, and so did his relationships. All it took was *giving up* the beliefs that were holding him back and it started with him being willing to explore and test this for himself. Through our conversations and with resources I directed him to, he dropped his old way of seeing things and saw through many of his own misunderstandings.

We can all do this. It's that simple. And in my personal and coaching experience I have seen that doing so has the greatest positive impact on our lives. Are you willing to let go of the beliefs, stories and ideas that are holding you back?

CHAPTER 53.

The Flow State Is Here, Now

I once coached a young lady who was a creative, artistic type. She enjoyed drawing and painting and felt she had lost the state of flow she once had that enabled her to do her best work. It seemed to her that that this state of flow, of clarity and infinite creativity was a place to get to. She thought it was a destination that could be reached by her doing things to clear her mind.

In the past, I too have had moments when I felt like I was in flow, or in the zone. These moments didn't seem to happen often, but I certainly could recall times when I was really creative and coming up with great ideas. I used to think this state depended on the time of day. I thought I got my best work done at night, although there were times it seemed to be first thing in the morning.

Sometimes it seemed like I tapped into this state more effectively when I'd had better sleep and rest. Yet there were times when the opposite was true—I would be running on very little sleep and still come up with great ideas. Still other times I could be well rested *or* dead tired and *not* come up with anything. In other words, this flow state seemed tricky to pin down—for myself in the past and for my client in the present.

What I realised, and what I pointed her to, was that this state was not somewhere to get *to*. In fact, it was her own misunderstanding about how the mind worked that was getting in the way of her returning to this state of flow. Just as children do, we have the ability to tap into infinite creativity, curiosity and joy. This is, in fact, our natural state, but we are so caught up in our misunderstandings that we don't spend anywhere near as much time in this state as we might do.

I pointed these things out to my client—that this state was her *natural* state, and that her efforts to get *to* it were actually getting in her way. She relaxed, her mind cleared and those thoughts—those roadblocks—fell away. She found herself in her creative element once again. The state "emerged" from within her—where it had been all along.

Realising this myself in recent years has helped me tremendously. For example, this book seemed to write itself. I have also found myself having many great ideas for my business without forcing myself to think about it or desperately seeking a state of flow.

The bottom line is that we are often busy in our own heads because we have misunderstandings about how our minds work, and how this affects our experience of life. This busy mind temporarily makes us lose sight of the underlying creativity and state of flow that is always within us.

CHAPTER 54.

You Don't Need to Avoid Boredom

In the year or two before I started training as a coach and was introduced to the understanding that I am sharing in this book, I constantly found myself bored. In order to avoid that feeling, I would distract myself. I downloaded the cult smartphone game *Angry Birds*. Every time I felt myself slipping into the feeling of boredom, I'd reach for my phone. Phew, thank God I avoided that feeling of boredom.

If the phone was not enough I would binge watch television programs. To mix it up, I could also avoid feeling bored by internet surfing for the most random of things—such as what other films an actor had been in or where to take my next holiday. Even worse, I could spend hours looking at other people's lives by getting sucked into the world of Facebook.

In my workplace, this avoidance of boredom would cause me to be less productive. I would actively avoid work that I thought was boring and gravitate towards work that I found interesting. I would often secretly hope that if I avoided the boring work long enough it would somehow magically disappear. It never occurred to me to ponder why, whenever I did set about doing what I thought was boring work, it was never as bad as I thought it would be.

I see now that boredom is simply a feeling, and as such it has nothing to do with the task I am performing, or with a lack of activity or stimulation. When I thought that it did, I would look for many things to distract me. Funnily enough, while they distracted me for a while, they often still didn't help me to stop feeling bored. If boredom as a feeling is simply a reflection of our thinking, then we don't need to do anything about it. The feeling of boredom is not good or bad; it's not something to be avoided. It is simply a reflection of our thinking in the moment, which can change at any second. It's not something we have to act upon.

Actually, the problem is not the feeling of boredom. The problem is us thinking that we shouldn't be feeling bored, that it's something to be avoided. Let's say I'm working at a "boring" task—does my feeling of being bored mean I need to stop? Our efforts to avoid the feeling are the real problem. They lead us to try to distract ourselves rather than just allowing ourselves to be okay—and perhaps bored—in the moment. The distractions we settle on can create their own problems. When I was distracting myself with binge-watching television, I became less mobile and more lethargic. I spent less time with my loved ones and even ate less healthy food. I created problems for myself simply by trying to avoid a feeling.

Our efforts to avoid boredom represent a huge misunderstanding that impacts many of us today. With social media, streaming television, smartphones and tablets we have more ways than ever of distracting ourselves out of a fear of boredom. If we see that this not only isn't necessary but actually doesn't make sense, we can be more productive, healthier and happier.

How would you behave differently if you didn't try to avoid feeling bored?

CHAPTER 55.

Love from Our Parents

As I mentioned in an earlier chapter, growing up I felt a powerful need for my father's appreciation. I think it's worth reiterating this point in a separate chapter, because our relationships with our parents can represent huge areas of misunderstanding for so many people. So it was for me. But when I came across the understanding I've been sharing in this book, this all changed. Today I have wonderful relationships with both my parents, for which I am very grateful.

As a teenager I felt, as I am sure many a teenager before me has done, that my parents didn't love me. I would look at their behaviour when I found it challenging to me and conclude that it was a result of them not loving me. Of course, I would feel upset and angry about this, and I would push them away and act out. So although I felt they didn't love me, at the same time, I craved their love. In fact, I wanted that more than anything else in the world because when I believed they didn't love me, I surmised that it meant I was not loveable.

Little did I know that this feeling could not be given to me by them. They could not create a feeling of parental love inside my mind—only I could do that. I believed it was theirs to give, but because I didn't feel it I judged them and their behaviour. It was the perfect recipe for a strained relationship.

I was recently talking to a divorced woman who told me that her son was constantly let down by her ex-husband making promises to him, which he then broke. She reached out to me for advice and described her situation and her options moving forward. It suddenly occurred to me that the mother was operating under a misunderstanding. She felt that on some level her son needed love from his father and, because his father was behaving the way he was, the son was missing out.

I told her that her son was perfect as he was. He would be okay no matter what happened in the future with her ex-husband. If her son was looking for a feeling of love from his father, that might inadvertently be pushing the father away—if he felt that his son had expectations he couldn't measure up to. I suggested that the best thing she could do for her son was to let him know that all the feelings he was looking for were never going to come from his father, from her, or from anyone or anything else. This was okay, because all those feelings had nothing to do with his father but everything to do with thought.

When I saw this for myself years earlier, my relationship with my own parents changed and I dropped years of judgement and misunderstanding. I was finally able to have a real, loving relationship with my parents without all the made-up thinking I had around them. Our parents do what they think is best given the thinking they have. It's not personal, and thankfully they ultimately have no power to make us feel anything at all. Believing they do is the misunderstanding that causes so many issues in relationships between parents and children. Now we may not fully understand—or be expected to understand this—when we're very young children. But thankfully, as time goes by we can open ourselves up to this new way of seeing the world, and set ourselves free. As someone once said, "It's never too late to have a happy childhood"

Would your relationship with your own parents change

(whether they are alive or not) if you had a real, embodied knowing that they were doing the best that they could in bringing you up and that, in all likelihood, if you were in their place and had the same thinking you would most likely behave in the same way?

CHAPTER 56.

Listening Is Easy

I was a terrible listener back in my twenties. This despite hearing axioms like "We're born with two ears and one mouth—so listen twice as much as you talk." When I tried implementing this strategy, I often found my conversations would stall. I'd end up in this awkward silence. I was often just listening because I thought I should—but I still wasn't really hearing what the other person was saying.

When I moved into coaching, in the back of my mind I was a little concerned. Coaches are supposedly excellent listeners, and I knew this wasn't a strong point of mine. When I started out, and was on calls with my clients, I would sometimes put my phone or computer mic on mute in order to stop myself from speaking over a client—something I noticed I had occasionally done. It was a strategy that had some minimal impact. What I found over time, however, was that the more deeply I understood the way we create our reality via our thinking, the more I was able to listen.

It is true that I still talk a lot. I wouldn't say that I am the best listener in the world. However, I *can* say that not only do I often talk less than I used to, but when I listen to someone, I am able to hear what they are saying much better than ever before. I used to simply wait for the other person in a conversation to take a breath so I could jump in with my point of view—hardly the mark of a great listener. More recently I have received compliments on my listening ability—something that I could never have imagined when I started coaching.

When we understand how the mind works, listening to and really hearing what another person has to say becomes much easier because it gives us context. If, for example, our friend is complaining about her boyfriend, knowing that she is creating that experience herself immediately allows us to hear her from a place of compassion; she is caught up in a misunderstanding, just as we have all been at one time or another. From that space we can really listen; we may not even feel the need to jump in and offer advice or tell her what to do.

The same holds true when our children want to talk with us about something that happened at school but we're busy with work. Having this framework of understanding in our minds makes it far easier for us to detect that this is important to them and stop what we are doing to listen. In this instance it makes it easier for us to let go of our thoughts and feelings about needing to get work done at that moment. We all know when someone is really listening to us—there is no way to fake it.

This is true in sales. How many times have you been speaking to a salesperson who clearly wasn't listening to what you had to say? Someone who was just trying to close a sale? If you're anything like me, this makes it far less likely you'll buy from that person. If, on the other hand, they were able to let go of their thought that they *had* to make a sale, it would be easier for them to listen—and the potential buyer would feel more comfortable with them and so be more likely to buy something.

Seeing how the world works means our minds are simply less busy with overthinking, analysing and confusion. With clearer minds we have a greater capacity to listen to another person. Wouldn't we all love to be listened to by someone else who had nothing on their minds? Or to give them the same gift of our pure, undivided attention?

CHAPTER 57.

How Do I Stop Thinking?

I get asked all the time: "How do I stop thinking?" We've already touched on this from different angles, but I want to address it again because it's so important.

My clients often think at the start of our work together that I am pointing them towards stopping their thoughts or at least encouraging them to stop certain unhelpful thoughts.

I am not.

Yes, having a clear mind is really helpful, but a clear mind is a by-product of seeing how we create our reality, rather than something we have to achieve.

There is no need to stop thinking once you understand how our mind works. For my part, I found that when I tried to stop thinking it was quite difficult for me. I really had very little control over my own thinking. I couldn't choose the thoughts that I had (and believe me I tried). In fact, I found that trying to control or stop my thinking often had the opposite effect from what I was looking for.

In the past, if I ever sat down to meditate or quiet my mind, I would find myself inundated with many different thoughts. The more I tried to quiet them down, the more they seemed to increase in frequency.

Now many people do meditate. If you're one of them, and you find that it is helpful to you, then by all means keep doing it!

It has been pointed out to me, however, that there is a difference between the *practice* of meditation and the *state* of meditation. At first I didn't understand the difference, but as my mind started to more frequently return to a quiet place on its own, I realised I was experiencing a *state* of meditation. I wasn't overthinking, analysing or trying to figure something out. It was very different for me from the times I had tried to practice meditation in the past, and in my case it came about as a result of my not trying to meddle with my thinking. My mind was quieter for longer periods of time as I dropped my misunderstandings about life. It started to settle down on its own. I realised that my mentors were correct when they told me that the mind's natural state is to be quiet.

Nowadays I experience a much quieter mind than I ever did previously. I am comfortable with and even enjoy silence.

I remember once being on a packed commuter train on my way home from work. There were no seats and everyone was squashed up against each other. No-one had the luxury of personal space on that journey and yet, in a situation where I would have previously been irritable (and many of my fellow commuters were), I fell into a very quiet mental place.

I truly believe that if a chronic overthinker like me can experience moments where my mind is extremely quiet, without engaging in a routine meditation practice, then it is possible for any human being.

As I have mentioned, a quiet mind is not a place to get to; it's a by-product of understanding how the mind works, of realising that we don't experience the world directly. We can't. We experience the world via our own thinking. Seeing this gives us greater perspective on our lives. On the flip side, a by-product of not understanding how the mind works, of having misunderstandings about life, is a noisy mind.

If a client of mine has a belief, a misunderstanding, that she can only be happy when she meets "Mr Right", then when she does in fact meet someone new she may think things like, "Is he the one?" "I like his confidence, but I wonder if he really likes me" "Am I coming off poorly?" Similarly, if a client has a misunderstanding, a belief, that he can only be happy when he has financial security which can only happen once he has £3 million in the bank, then he will have a lot of thinking about money and decisions to take around it. "Should I invest now or should I hold off?" "What if I make this decision and I lose everything" "If I sleep two hours less a night, will I get to my goal quicker?"

These thoughts may be totally valid but through the lens of misunderstanding they take on an urgency that can interfere with our ability to perform naturally—and at our best. If the good feelings of love, approval and self-worth are dependant on Mr Right, then there is a pressure placed on meeting "the one", and urgent thinking comes as a result. The same is true with any misunderstanding we may have—it comes with the territory.

I feel as a young boy I intuitively spent time in a quiet state of mind, as all very young children do. I had fewer misunderstandings as a child—as likely did you. When I lost sight of this I would get angry or upset, but I always came back to this mental state of clarity. As I grew up, I forgot how my mind worked—like most of us do. I took on certain beliefs, ideas and misunderstandings—"I am a shy person," or "I'm not confident" or "This is simply how I am." These misunderstandings led to a busy mind, insecurities and an inflated ego. Once I started to remember how my mind worked and got out of my own way, these insecurities began falling away, and I started to recover my childlike wisdom.

Just as my clients do.

And just as you can too.

CHAPTER 58.

The Promise of a Life Lived from a New Understanding

This final chapter is really one of hope.

I don't expect that after you've read this book all the changes that have occurred in the past six years of my life will immediately occur for you too. Many of them happened gradually for me as this new understanding spread through all the different areas of my life (and the process is still unfolding). However, I would love to open you up to the possibility of the real, drastic and permanent change that can take place when we see how the world and our own minds really work.

This book, then, is a message of hope for radical personal transformation. I don't mean hope in terms of wishing and praying that circumstances will change. I also don't mean it in terms of thinking that your feelings will change and you will never feel bad. Your circumstances are your circumstances and you often have little control over them or exactly what you're thinking and feeling. The good news is that your circumstances don't impact how you feel, and all thoughts and feelings are transient—as long as we don't hold on to them. Once this understanding becomes clear and active within you, life gets a whole lot simpler. By not buying into your misunderstandings, a whole new world of possibility and potential opens up.

I've shared some of the changes that I and my clients have

experienced because I want you to see the truth of what I am pointing to for yourself. I want you to see the myriad of changes that are possible for you. My intention was to fill this book with numerous examples of the implications of deepening your understanding of the mind. It can be easy to assume that the fact that our feelings are a reflection of our thinking in the moment is not a big deal. But really seeing this new paradigm can stop us from creating unnecessary issues for ourselves and bring us back to our innate mental health and wellbeing.

You don't need to take my word for it. Simply let this book be a doorway into further exploration and find out for yourself.

I know for myself that the changes I have experienced over the past six years are not the end of my own journey. Even during the process of writing this book, I have had insights and realisations and seen changes in my own life. Each day, there is the possibility of seeing something deeper than I have seen it already—and with it the potential for further transformation.

This gives me incredible hope not only for my own life but also for everyone else on this planet. This may sound grandiose but I have seen so many lives changed beyond what people thought possible that I know the potential exists for *everyone*. As I have mentioned elsewhere, if my life can change to the degree that it has, then I know it is absolutely possible for everyone else. It certainly is possible for you.

They say that only a fool tries to change the world. Perhaps I am a little foolish, perhaps not.

I don't know anyone who has explored the nature of the mind who hasn't been glad they did so. Perhaps this book has you intrigued enough to continue your own journey towards understanding how the mind really works. Perhaps it will serve as a reminder of what is really possible for you.

It is normal to forget, but I hope this book reminds you of who you really are.

The perfect you who was there the moment you were born.

Acknowledgements

I want to express my heartfelt appreciation to the following:

- To Sydney Banks who had a profound realisation of the foundations of human psychological functioning which inspired a fundamentally new paradigm in psychology.
- To Steve Chandler, my coach, who first helped me see I had something worth writing about and who provided valuable insights in making this book a reality.
- To Yamini Jain, my wife, for being one of my first two proofreaders and supporting me in sharing my message. In it together!
- To Keith Blevens and Valda Monroe for having the greatest impact on my own understanding of how the human mind works, for the single paradigm and for your continued friendship and support.
- To Dicken Bettinger for helping me see the power of silence and explaining that there are three principles.
- To Chip and Jan Chipman for the mentoring, friendship and guidance.
- To Elsie Spittle for your friendship, support and guidance.
- To Linda Quiring for reading my manuscript, encouraging me and supporting this project.
- To Mark Howard for pointing me to simply share what I know. Thank you for your support, guidance and

friendship.
- To Jamie Smart for first pointing me to the principles which underpin this book and my coaching.
- To Aaron Turner for your continued guidance, friendship and pointing out the importance of our own grounding.
- To Cheryl Bond for supporting me in delivering my first ever training in this understanding and your continued friendship.
- To Cathy Casey for supporting me on the women's immersion training programs and your continued friendship and guidance.
- To Chantal Burns for your continued friendship and advice to make this a better book.
- To Amy Johnson for helping me drop my own thinking about the 3P police.
- To Garret Kramer for your teaching and encouragement in those early days.
- To John Epstein for helping me redefine the word success and everything that it subsequently led to. I appreciate your continued friendship and support.
- To Zan Perrion for the Ars Amorata and changing the course of my life.
- To Abdul Amin for first introducing me to the world of personal development.
- To Henk Kok for inspiring me to finally start my book.
- To all of my clients I have coached, past and present.
- To all of my colleagues who have been so incredibly supportive of my work.
- To Kristi Palma for method writing.
- To Chris Nelson for editing this book.
- To Maurice Bassett for your honest feedback which led to making this a better book.
- To my parents, who are my biggest supporters.

Further Reading

These are the books I most frequently recommend to (and often purchase for) my clients, friends and family. Many of these books greatly inspired this one, and I highly recommend them if you are interested in more deeply understanding how the mind really works.

The Missing Link: Reflections on Philosophy and Spirit by Sydney Banks (Lone Pine Publishing, 1998)

Instant Motivation: The Surprising Truth Behind What Really Drives Top Performance by Chantal Burns (Pearson, 2014)

Invisible Power: Insight Principles at Work by Ken Manning, Robin Charbit and Sandra Krot (Insight Principles, 2015)

The Inside-Out Revolution: The Only Thing You Need to Know to Change Your Life Forever by Michael Neill (Hay House, 2013)

The Relationship Handbook: A Simple Guide to Satisfying Relationships by George S. Pransky Ph.D. (Pransky and Associates, 2017)

Somebody Should Have Told Us!: Simple Truths for Living Well by Jack Pransky (CCB Publishing, 2011)

Island of Knowledge by Linda Quiring (CCB Publishing, 2015)

The Little Book of Clarity by Jamie Smart (Wiley, 2015)

About the Author

Ankush is a life coach, public speaker and trainer based in the UK with clients from Australia to Canada.

Ankush is the founder of the Powerful Men's Group and has run multiple sold out Powerful Men's Immersions in the UK several times a year since 2015. As well as this he coaches other coaches to develop their practices through deeply impactful coaching with a focus on service.

He was the host of the successful Relationship Series podcast and in 2018 started the new Business Series Podcast aimed at a corporate audience.

Ankush lives in London with his wife Yamini.

You can find out more about what he is up to at:

www.ankushjain.co.uk

CPSIA information can be obtained
at www.ICGtesting.com
Printed in the USA
LVHW051735080719
623457LV00015B/332